THE BRYANT ADVANTAGE

Binary, Subnetting and Summarization Mastery

CHRIS BRYANT

Copyright @2018 The Bryant Advantage, Inc.

All rights reserved. This book or any portion thereof may not be reproduced or used in any manner whatsoever without the express written permission of the publisher except for the use of brief quotations in a book review.

No part of this publication may be stored in a retrieval system, transmitted, or reproduced in any way, including but not limited to photocopy, photograph, magnetic, or other record, without the prior agreement and written permission of the publisher.

The Bryant Advantage, Inc., has attempted throughout this book to distinguish proprietary trademarks from descriptive terms by following the capitalization style used by the manufacturer. Copyrights and trademarks of all products and services listed or described herein are property of their respective owners and companies. All rules and laws pertaining to said copyrights and trademarks are inferred.

Life comes at you fast. I'm going to make him an offer he can't refuse. Here's looking at you, kid. Go ahead, make my day. Coffee is for closers. He's convinced me, gimme back my dollar! You plan a good enough getaway, you could steal Ebbets Field. It was a run-by fruiting! If you want me to keep my mouth shut, it's gonna cost you some dough. I figure a thousand bucks is reasonable, so I want two.

Finally, even the darkest night will end and the sun will rise.

Printed in the United States of America. First printing, 2018

Table of Contents

CHAPTER 1: A (Very) Quick Introductory Chapter 5

CHAPTER 2: Converting Binary Strings To Dotted Decimal 7

CHAPTER 3: Binary-to-Decimal Conversion Exercises 11

CHAPTER 4: Converting Decimals To Binary Strings 17

CHAPTER 5: Decimal-to-Binary Conversion Exercises 23

CHAPTER 6: Determining The Number Of Valid Subnets 29

CHAPTER 7: "Number of Valid Subnets" Exercises 35

CHAPTER 8: Determining The Number Of Valid Hosts On A Subnet 41

CHAPTER 9: "Number Of Valid Hosts Per Subnet" Exercises 45

CHAPTER 10: Determining The Subnet Of An IP Address 53

CHAPTER 11: IP Address Subnet Exercises 57

CHAPTER 12: Determining A Subnet's Broadcast Address and Range Of Valid Addresses 61

CHAPTER 13: Broadcast Number / Valid Address Range Exercises 65

CHAPTER 14: Subnetting, Actually 75

CHAPTER 15: Subnetting Scenarios 79

CHAPTER 16: Son Of Subnetting Situations 85

CHAPTER 17: Subnetting Situations III 91

CHAPTER 18: Variable-Length Subnet Masking (VLSM) 99

CHAPTER 19: VLSM Exercises 107

CHAPTER 20: Manual Route Summarization 129

CHAPTER 21: Bonus Review Exercise Set #1 139

CHAPTER 22: Bonus Review Exercise Set #2: 145

CHAPTER 23: Bonus Review Exercise Set #3 153

CHAPTER 1:

A (Very) Quick Introductory Chapter

Hi there!

Thanks for picking up this copy of *Binary, Subnetting, and Summarization Mastery*. Whether you're brand new to all three of these skills, need a refresher, or you're somewhere in between, this book is *guaranteed* to help you master the skills needed for both today's Cisco and CompTIA certification exams and real-world networking.

When you follow the structured path I've created for you and practice with the exercises in this book, you're going to become a world-class subnetter and subnetting troubleshooter. There's no doubt about it. *Nothing* can stop you.

Not only will you be able to perform subnetting from the very beginning (more on that in Chapter 14), you'll be able to analyze subnetting performed by others to see how many valid subnets their subnetting resulted in, as well as how many valid host addresses exist on that subnet.

These are skills you'll find very helpful on exam day, and you'll use them in your real-life networking jobs, both present and future.

I've included three bonus chapters of practice questions in this edition, so you have plenty of practice ahead – and that's the real "secret" to mastering both subnetting and summarization. Practice.

If you have any questions, compliments, comments, or complaints regarding this book, please share them with me via the links below.

Thanks for making my work a part of your success story!

Chris Bryant

CCIE #12933

"The Computer Certification Bulldog"

Website: https://www.thebryantadvantage.com

Twitter: https://www.twitter.com/ccie12933

Facebook: https://www.facebook.com/ccie12933/

LinkedIn: https://www.linkedin.com/in/bulldogchrisbryant/

YouTube: https://www.youtube.com/user/ccie12933

CCNA Video Boot Camp: http://bit.ly/CCNA2019

Subnetting Success Exam Pack: http://bit.ly/SubnetSuccess

CHAPTER 2:

Converting Binary Strings To Dotted Decimal

We'll dive right in with a short binary string, 01101101, and convert it to a decimal. You'll need this very short little chart:

128	64	32	16	8	4	2	1

There's absolutely no need to draw the entire grid out when you're taking the exam. I'm putting the grid lines in here to make it easier to follow. And if this is new to you, note that all you're doing here is starting with the number one on the far right and then doubling it seven times. Once you get some practice in, you'll write those numbers out without even thinking about it.

When you're converting binary to decimal, all you have to do is write that string out as it's given to you, one bit at a time, like this:

128	64	32	16	8	4	2	1
0	1	1	0	1	1	0	1

Add up the values that have a "1" under them, and you have your decimal. The sum of 64, 32, 8, 4, and 1 is 109. If you can do this conversion – and you just did – you can solve any subnetting question *anyone* gives you.

If you're given a binary string that has four separate octets, just convert each 8-bit string separately. Let's use the binary string 11110000 00110111 11001100 00000011 for some practice.

	128	64	32	16	8	4	2	1
Octet 1	1	1	1	1	0	0	0	0
Octet 2	0	0	1	1	0	1	1	1
Octet 3	1	1	0	0	1	1	0	0
Octet 4	0	0	0	0	0	0	1	1

Add up each row separately, and you get 240, 55, 204, and 3, which represents the IP address 240.55.204.3. That's all there is to this important skill.

Let's tackle five more practice questions. I'll give you the five questions first, and the answers begin immediately afterward.

Question 1: Convert the string 11110001 00110101 11100011 00101011 to dotted decimal.

Question 2: What IP address is represented by the string 00111000 00110011 10101010 11111110?

Question 3: Convert the string 11110001 to dotted decimal.

Question 4: What IP address is represented by the string 11110010 00100101 11011011 11000000?

Question 5: Convert the string 11001010 to dotted decimal.

And now... the answers!

Answer 1: *Convert the string 11110001 00110101 11100011 00101011 to dotted decimal.*

The address is 241.53.227.43.

128	64	32	16	8	4	2	1	**TOTAL**
1	1	1	1	0	0	0	1	**241**
0	0	1	1	0	1	0	1	**53**
1	1	1	0	0	0	1	1	**227**
0	0	1	0	1	0	1	1	**43**

Answer 2: *What IP address is represented by the string 00111000 00110011 10101010 11111110?*

The address is 56.51.170.254.

128	64	32	16	8	4	2	1	**TOTAL**
0	0	1	1	1	0	0	0	**56**
0	0	1	1	0	0	1	1	**51**
1	0	1	0	1	0	1	0	**170**
1	1	1	1	1	1	1	0	**254**

Answer 3: Convert the string 11110001 to dotted decimal.

The decimal is 241.

128	64	32	16	8	4	2	1	**TOTAL**
1	1	1	1	0	0	0	1	**241**

Answer 4: What IP address is represented by the string 11110010 00100101 11011011 11000000?

The address is 242.37.219.192.

128	64	32	16	8	4	2	1	**TOTAL**
1	1	1	1	0	0	1	0	**242**
0	0	1	0	0	1	0	1	**37**
1	1	0	1	1	0	1	1	**219**
1	1	0	0	0	0	0	0	**192**

Answer 5: Convert the string 11001010 to dotted decimal.

The dotted decimal is 202.

128	64	32	16	8	4	2	1	**TOTAL**
1	1	0	0	1	0	1	0	**202**

Success with binary and subnetting is all about practice, so I have an additional practice section for you following this chapter. After that, we'll hit decimal-to-binary conversions. Let's get to it!

CHAPTER 3:

Binary-to-Decimal Conversion Exercises

Convert 01011111 00100101 10011000 00101111 to dotted decimal.

128	**64**	**32**	**16**	**8**	**4**	**2**	**1**	Total
0	1	0	1	1	1	1	1	95
0	0	1	0	0	1	0	1	37
1	0	0	1	1	0	0	0	152
0	0	1	0	1	1	1	1	47

Convert 01100011 10000100 10010011 11010110 to dotted decimal.

128	**64**	**32**	**16**	**8**	**4**	**2**	**1**	Total
0	1	1	0	0	0	1	1	99
1	0	0	0	0	1	0	0	132
1	0	0	1	0	0	1	1	147
1	1	0	1	0	1	1	0	214

Convert 01010100 01111001 11001011 00110110 to dotted decimal.

128	**64**	**32**	**16**	**8**	**4**	**2**	**1**	Total
0	1	0	1	0	1	0	0	84
0	1	1	1	1	0	0	1	121
1	1	0	0	1	0	1	1	203
0	0	1	1	0	1	1	0	54

Convert 00010101 01001001 10011001 11100010 to dotted decimal.

128	64	32	16	8	4	2	1	Total
0	0	0	1	0	1	0	1	21
0	1	0	0	1	0	0	1	73
1	0	0	1	1	0	0	1	153
1	1	1	0	0	0	1	0	226

Convert 11110100 00100110 00111101 10100001 to dotted decimal.

128	64	32	16	8	4	2	1	Total
1	1	1	1	0	1	0	0	244
0	0	1	0	0	1	1	0	38
0	0	1	1	1	1	0	1	61
1	0	1	0	0	0	0	1	161

Convert 00010001 01000001 11111011 10110001 to dotted decimal.

128	64	32	16	8	4	2	1	Total
0	0	0	1	0	0	0	1	17
0	1	0	0	0	0	0	1	65
1	1	1	1	1	0	1	1	251
1	0	1	1	0	0	0	1	177

Convert 00111011 01010111 11011011 01111111 to dotted decimal.

128	64	32	16	8	4	2	1	Total
0	0	1	1	1	0	1	1	59
0	1	0	1	0	1	1	1	87
1	1	0	1	1	0	1	1	219
0	1	1	1	1	1	1	1	127

Convert 01001101 10101000 00010011 10001101 to dotted decimal.

128	64	32	16	8	4	2	1	Total
0	1	0	0	1	1	0	1	77
1	0	1	0	1	0	0	0	168
0	0	0	1	0	0	1	1	19
1	0	0	0	1	1	0	1	141

Convert 11010001 10010001 00011011 00101011 to dotted decimal.

128	64	32	16	8	4	2	1	Total
1	1	0	1	0	0	0	1	209
1	0	0	1	0	0	0	1	145
0	0	0	1	1	0	1	1	27
0	0	1	0	1	0	1	1	43

Convert 10110011 00100011 11111010 01001111 to dotted decimal.

128	64	32	16	8	4	2	1	Total
1	0	1	1	0	0	1	1	179
0	0	1	0	0	0	1	1	35
1	1	1	1	1	0	1	0	250
0	1	0	0	1	1	1	1	79

Convert 01100110 10011010 00110101 11110101 to dotted decimal.

128	64	32	16	8	4	2	1	Total
0	1	1	0	0	1	1	0	102
1	0	0	1	1	0	1	0	154
0	0	1	1	0	1	0	1	53
1	1	1	1	0	1	0	1	245

Convert 10110100 01110011 11000101 11101010 to dotted decimal.

128	64	32	16	8	4	2	1	Total
1	0	1	1	0	1	0	0	180
0	1	1	1	0	0	1	1	115
1	1	0	0	0	1	0	1	197
1	1	1	0	1	0	1	0	234

Convert 01110111 00011001 10001011 10110100 to dotted decimal.

128	64	32	16	8	4	2	1	Total
0	1	1	1	0	1	1	1	119
0	0	0	1	1	0	0	1	25
1	0	0	0	1	0	1	1	139
1	0	1	1	0	1	0	0	180

Convert 10111100 00001110 01110101 10111111 to dotted decimal.

128	64	32	16	8	4	2	1	Total
1	0	1	1	1	1	0	0	188
0	0	0	0	1	1	1	0	14
0	1	1	1	0	1	0	1	117
1	0	1	1	1	1	1	1	191

Convert 11011100 11110000 01010000 01111101 to dotted decimal.

128	64	32	16	8	4	2	1	Total
1	1	0	1	1	1	0	0	220
1	1	1	1	0	0	0	0	240
0	1	0	1	0	0	0	0	80
0	1	1	1	1	1	0	1	125

Convert 01011011 10111000 01000010 00101100 to dotted decimal.

128	64	32	16	8	4	2	1	Total
0	1	0	1	1	0	1	1	91
1	0	1	1	1	0	0	0	184
0	1	0	0	0	0	1	0	66
0	0	1	0	1	1	0	0	44

Convert 10100101 11001111 01101001 11001111 to dotted decimal.

128	64	32	16	8	4	2	1	Total
1	0	1	0	0	1	0	1	165
1	1	0	0	1	1	1	1	207
0	1	1	0	1	0	0	1	105
1	1	0	0	1	1	1	1	207

Convert 01111101 00110001 10101011 10001000 to dotted decimal.

128	64	32	16	8	4	2	1	Total
0	1	1	1	1	1	0	1	125
0	0	1	1	0	0	0	1	49
1	0	1	0	1	0	1	1	171
1	0	0	0	1	0	0	0	136

Convert 11000011 01011000 00011101 01100100 to dotted decimal.

128	64	32	16	8	4	2	1	Total
1	1	0	0	0	0	1	1	195
0	1	0	1	1	0	0	0	88
0	0	0	1	1	1	0	1	29
0	1	1	0	0	1	0	0	100

Convert 10010101 11100001 00010010 10101111 to dotted decimal.

128	64	32	16	8	4	2	1	Total
1	0	0	1	0	1	0	1	149
1	1	1	0	0	0	0	1	225
0	0	0	1	0	0	1	0	18
1	0	1	0	1	1	1	1	175

I know that was a lot of practice with one particular skill, and it's practice that will pay off as we progress through the book. Nice work! Now it's time to tackle decimal-to-binary conversions.

CHAPTER 4:

Converting Decimals To Binary Strings

We're going to use this skill quite often in subnetting, and we're pretty much doing the same thing we did in the previous section – just in reverse.

Makes perfect sense, right?   I promise it'll make sense after we run through a few drills. This is one of those skills that seems really complicated when you read about it, but when you actually do it, you realize how easy it is. Let's get some practice with the decimal 217.

	128	64	32	16	8	4	2	1
217								

All we have to do is determine whether each bit should be set to one or zero, and it's a simple two-step process (with three bullet points).

- Work from left to right and ask this one question: "Can I subtract this column's value from the current octet value with the result being a positive number or a zero?"

- If the answer is *yes*, perform the subtraction, put a "1" in the column, and go to the next column and repeat using the remainder.

- If the answer is *no*, place a "0" in the column and repeat the process for the next column.

It takes much longer to explain this operation than to actually do it, so let's do it!

	128	64	32	16	8	4	2	1
217								

Can 128 be subtracted from 217 and result in a positive number or zero? Sure! 217 − 128 = 89. Put a "1" in the 128 column and head to the next column. Repeat the operation with the *new remainder.*

	128	64	32	16	8	4	2	1
217	1							

Can 64 be subtracted from 89? Yes. 89 − 64 = 25. Put a "1" in the 64 column and move on to the next column, carrying that 25 with you as you go.

	128	64	32	16	8	4	2	1
217	1	1						

Can 32 be subtracted from 25? No. You'd end up with a negative number, so put a zero in that column and move on to the next.

	128	64	32	16	8	4	2	1
217	1	1	0					

Can 16 be subtracted from 25? Yes. 25 − 16 = 9. Put a "1" in the 16 column and move on with that 9.

	128	64	32	16	8	4	2	1
217	1	1	0	1				

We can subtract 8 from 9 with no problem. 9 − 8 = 1, so we move forward with a remainder of 1 after putting a "1" in the 8 column.

	128	64	32	16	8	4	2	1
217	1	1	0	1	1			

We know darn well you can't subtract 4 or 2 from 1 without ending up with a negative number. Put zeroes under those two columns. Finally, we subtract 1 from 1, and we have zero. Put a "1" in the 1 column, and we're done.

	128	64	32	16	8	4	2	1
217	1	1	0	1	1	0	0	1

The decimal 217 is represented by the binary string 11011001.

If either of the two following things happens, your conversion is off, and you need to do it again:

- You have a remainder after filling in the "1" bit.

- You have the number 2 under one of those bits instead of one or zero. If you do that, you have reinvented binary, and we would appreciate it if you would not do that.

In all seriousness, if you have a remainder or a two, you gotta do it again. Let's get some more work in on this conversion type by converting each of the following IP addresses to a binary string. You're doing the exact same thing you did with the single decimal 217; you're just doing it four times per address. Answers follow the questions.

- 100.10.1.200
- 190.4.89.23
- 11.255.18.244
- 240.17.23.239
- 217.34.39.214

No peeking at...the answers!

Conversion 1: 100.10.1.200

The string: 01100100 00001010 00000001 11001000.

	128	64	32	16	8	4	2	1
100	0	1	1	0	0	1	0	0
10	0	0	0	0	1	0	1	0
1	0	0	0	0	0	0	0	1
200	1	1	0	0	1	0	0	0

Conversion 2: 190.4.89.23

The string: 10111110   00000100   01011001   00010111.

	128	64	32	16	8	4	2	1
190	1	0	1	1	1	1	1	0
4	0	0	0	0	0	1	0	0
89	0	1	0	1	1	0	0	1
23	0	0	0	1	0	1	1	1

Conversion 3: 11.255.18.244

The string: 00001011   11111111   00010010   11110100.

	128	64	32	16	8	4	2	1
11	0	0	0	0	1	0	1	1
255	1	1	1	1	1	1	1	1
18	0	0	0	1	0	0	1	0
244	1	1	1	1	0	1	0	0

Conversion 4: 240.17.23.239

The string: 11110000   00010001   00010111   11101111.

	128	64	32	16	8	4	2	1
240	1	1	1	1	0	0	0	0
17	0	0	0	1	0	0	0	1
23	0	0	0	1	0	1	1	1
239	1	1	1	0	1	1	1	1

Conversion 5: 217.34.39.214

The string: 11011001   00100010   00100111   11010110.

	128	64	32	16	8	4	2	1
217	1	1	0	1	1	0	0	1
34	0	0	1	0	0	0	1	0
39	0	0	1	0	0	1	1	1
214	1	1	0	1	0	1	1	0

Let's get some more work in with this skill in the next chapter and then move on to our first subnetting scenarios.

CHAPTER 5:

Decimal-to-Binary Conversion Exercises

Convert the following dotted decimal addresses to binary.
- 38.47.89.211
- 177.58.40.227
- 133.49.77.241
- 89.148.222.13
- 135.99.81.197

38.47.89.211: 00100110 00101111 01011001 11010011

	128	64	32	16	8	4	2	1
38	0	0	1	0	0	1	1	0
47	0	0	1	0	1	1	1	1
89	0	1	0	1	1	0	0	1
211	1	1	0	1	0	0	1	1

177.58.40.227: 10110001 00111010 00101000 11100011

	128	64	32	16	8	4	2	1
177	1	0	1	1	0	0	0	1
58	0	0	1	1	1	0	1	0
40	0	0	1	0	1	0	0	0
227	1	1	1	0	0	0	1	1

133.49.77.241: 10000101 00110001 01001101 11110001

	128	64	32	16	8	4	2	1
133	1	0	0	0	0	1	0	1
49	0	0	1	1	0	0	0	1
77	0	1	0	0	1	1	0	1
241	1	1	1	1	0	0	0	1

89.148.222.13: 01011001 10010100 11011110 00001101

	128	64	32	16	8	4	2	1
89	0	1	0	1	1	0	0	1
148	1	0	0	1	0	1	0	0
222	1	1	0	1	1	1	1	0
13	0	0	0	0	1	1	0	1

135.99.81.197: 10000111 01100011 01010001 11000101

	128	64	32	16	8	4	2	1
135	1	0	0	0	0	1	1	1
99	0	1	1	0	0	0	1	1
81	0	1	0	1	0	0	0	1
197	1	1	0	0	0	1	0	1

Got five more for you. Keep grinding!
- 82.41.39.113
- 125.58.170.247
- 138.23.98.159
- 163.42.143.68
- 88.77.66.153

82.41.39.113:   01010010 00101001 00100111 01110001

	128	64	32	16	8	4	2	1
82	0	1	0	1	0	0	1	0
41	0	0	1	0	1	0	0	1
39	0	0	1	0	0	1	1	1
113	0	1	1	1	0	0	0	1

125.58.170.247:   01111101 00111010 10101010 11110111

	128	64	32	16	8	4	2	1
125	0	1	1	1	1	1	0	1
58	0	0	1	1	1	0	1	0
170	1	0	1	0	1	0	1	0
247	1	1	1	1	0	1	1	1

138.23.98.159:   10001010 00010111 01100010 10011111

	128	64	32	16	8	4	2	1
138	1	0	0	0	1	0	1	0
23	0	0	0	1	0	1	1	1
98	0	1	1	0	0	0	1	0
159	1	0	0	1	1	1	1	1

163.42.143.68:   10100011 00101010 10001111 01000100

	128	64	32	16	8	4	2	1
163	1	0	1	0	0	0	1	1
42	0	0	1	0	1	0	1	0
143	1	0	0	0	1	1	1	1
68	0	1	0	0	0	1	0	0

88.77.66.153:   01011000 01001101 01000010 10011001

	128	64	32	16	8	4	2	1
88	0	1	0	1	1	0	0	0
77	0	1	0	0	1	1	0	1
66	0	1	0	0	0	0	1	0
153	1	0	0	1	1	0	0	1

Five more!

- 83.211.49.243
- 47.39.200.148
- 100.200.139.55
- 39.219.177.89
- 244.33.121.182

83.211.49.243: 01010011 11010011 00110001 11110011

	128	64	32	16	8	4	2	1
83	0	1	0	1	0	0	1	1
211	1	1	0	1	0	0	1	1
49	0	0	1	1	0	0	0	1
243	1	1	1	1	0	0	1	1

47.39.200.148: 00101111 00100111 11001000   10010100

	128	64	32	16	8	4	2	1
47	0	0	1	0	1	1	1	1
39	0	0	1	0	0	1	1	1
200	1	1	0	0	1	0	0	0
148	1	0	0	1	0	1	0	0

100.200.139.55:   01100100 11001000 10001011 00110111

	128	64	32	16	8	4	2	1
100	0	1	1	0	0	1	0	0
200	1	1	0	0	1	0	0	0
139	1	0	0	0	1	0	1	1
55	0	0	1	1	0	1	1	1

39.219.177.89:   00100111 11011011 10110001 01011001

	128	64	32	16	8	4	2	1
39	0	0	1	0	0	1	1	1
219	1	1	0	1	1	0	1	1
177	1	0	1	1	0	0	0	1
89	0	1	0	1	1	0	0	1

244.33.121.182:   11110100 00100001 01111001 10110110

	128	64	32	16	8	4	2	1
244	1	1	1	1	0	1	0	0
33	0	0	1	0	0	0	0	1
121	0	1	1	1	1	0	0	1
182	1	0	1	1	0	1	1	0

Just four more!

- 99.131.40.147
- 25.50.75.100
- 33.66.99.122
- 155.242.13.29

99.131.40.147: 01100011 10000011 00101000 10010011

	128	64	32	16	8	4	2	1
99	0	1	1	0	0	0	1	1
131	1	0	0	0	0	0	1	1
40	0	0	1	0	1	0	0	0
147	1	0	0	1	0	0	1	1

25.50.75.100: 00011001 00110010 01001011 01100100

	128	64	32	16	8	4	2	1
25	0	0	0	1	1	0	0	1
50	0	0	1	1	0	0	1	0
75	0	1	0	0	1	0	1	1
100	0	1	1	0	0	1	0	0

33.66.99.122: 00100001 01000010 01100011 01111010

	128	64	32	16	8	4	2	1
33	0	0	1	0	0	0	0	1
66	0	1	0	0	0	0	1	0
99	0	1	1	0	0	0	1	1
122	0	1	1	1	1	0	1	0

155.242.13.29: 10011011 11110010 00001101 00011101

	128	64	32	16	8	4	2	1
155	1	0	0	1	1	0	1	1
242	1	1	1	1	0	0	1	0
13	0	0	0	0	1	1	0	1
29	0	0	0	1	1	1	0	1

Great work! Coming up next, we'll learn the vital skill of calculating the number of valid subnets in an already-created subnetting scheme.

CHAPTER 6:

Determining The Number Of Valid Subnets

You definitely want to double-check and triple-check the number of valid subnets available in your addressing scheme *before* you start assigning addresses on your network. This is a valuable skill to have regardless of who did the actual subnetting, so in our walkthroughs and practice questions, we'll be presented with the already-subnetted network and then determine how many valid subnets we have to work with.

With practice, you'll answer "valid subnet" questions on your exams and in real-world networking situations in less than a minute.

Let's start our practice with these sample questions:

- *How many valid subnets are on the 10.0.0.0 255.240.0.0 network?*
- *How many valid subnets are on the 10.0.0.0 /12 network?*

These two questions are referring to the exact same network; they're just using different formats of expressing the subnet mask. The first uses a dotted decimal mask, while the second uses prefix notation. You're much more likely to see prefix notation than the dotted decimal mask in production networks and on network maps, but be ready for both formats on exam day.

With prefix notation, the number behind the slash is the number of consecutive ones at the beginning of the mask. The dotted decimal mask 255.240.0.0 converts to this binary string:

11111111   11110000   00000000   00000000

There are 12 ones at the start of that mask, and that's where the /12 comes from. Using prefix notation saves a lot of space on network diagrams and makes them easier to read, and it's a *lot* easier to discuss masks verbally using prefix notation.

Remember the Class A, B, and C network masks? Here's a quick review:

	Class A	Class B	Class C
1st Octet Range	1 – 126	128 – 191	192 – 223
Network Mask	255.0.0.0	255.255.0.0	255.255.255.0

Those network masks tell us how many network bits and host bits are present in each. Ones are network bits; zeroes are host bits.

Class A mask = 255.0.0.0 = 8 network bits, 24 host bits

Class B mask = 255.255.0.0 = 16 network bits, 16 host bits

Class C mask = 255.255.255.0 = 24 network bits, 8 host bits

Why do we care about the network bits and host bits? For this simple reason:

Subnetting is performed by borrowing host bits ONLY.

That's it. That's all subnetting is. You're borrowing host bits, and never, ever, ever network bits.

Let's go back to our practice question: *How many valid subnets are on the 10.0.0.0 /12 network?* The challenge here is that someone else has already done the subnetting, and we have to determine how many valid subnets now exist. I'm going to show you two methods for nailing these questions. The first method is longer but gives you a better idea of what exactly is happening with subnets and where the host bit borrowing comes in. The second method is quicker, and I suggest you use it only once you're comfortable with the first method.

For the longer method, we'll make a bit-by-bit comparison of the Class A network mask and the subnet mask /12. The subnet bits are the bits where there's a zero in the network mask and a one in the subnet mask.

	Octet 1	Octet 2	Octet 3	Octet 4
Network Mask	11111111	**0000**0000	00000000	00000000
Subnet Mask	11111111	**1111**0000	00000000	00000000

The subnet mask has eight network bits, four subnet bits, and 20 host bits. All we have to do is plug the number of subnet bits into this handy-dandy formula:

Number of valid subnets = (2 to the power of the number of subnet bits)

Sounds hard, right? Wrong! For 2 to the 4th power, we just multiply 2 by itself four times – 2 x 2 x 2 x 2, that is – and the result is 16. We have 16 valid subnets, and that's all there is to it.

Now that you see exactly what's going on with those borrowed bits, let me show you how to solve these questions without writing the masks out, using this question:

How many valid subnets are on the 150.10.0.0 /21 network?

This is where having your Class A, B, and C ranges and masks down cold will save you huge amounts of time on exam day. (Not to mention scoring easy points.) You know these two things about this network immediately:

- It's a Class B network
- The Class B network mask is /16

Just subtract the 16 bits of the network mask from the 21 bits in the subnet mask, and you have the number of subnet bits; in this case, 5. Take 2 to the 5th power – 2 x 2 x 2 x 2 x 2 – and you know how many valid subnets you have. 2 to the 5th power is 32, so you have 32 valid subnets.

This is a great skill to practice when you have just a few minutes to study something – just write out a network and subnet mask without thinking about it, like this…

200.1.1.0 /27

… and practice away. That's a class C network, so subtract 24 (the number of network bits in a Class C mask) from the subnet mask of /27, leaving you three subnet bits. 2 x 2 x 2 = 8 valid subnets. Done and done!

Let's get in some more work with valid subnet calculations with the following five networks.

- 15.0.0.0 /13
- 222.10.1.0 /30
- 145.45.0.0 /25
- 20.0.0.0 255.192.0.0
- 130.30.0.0 255.255.224.0

In the answers, I've written out the NW and SN masks. You don't have to write them out if you're comfortable with the quicker method. Subnet bits are bolded.

15.0.0.0 /13: It's a Class A network, so we have 8 network bits. Subnet mask is /13. 13 – 8 = 5 subnet bits, and 2 to the 5th power = 32 valid subnets.

| NW Mask | 11111111 | 00000000 | 00000000 | 00000000 |
| SN Mask | 11111111 | **11111**000 | 00000000 | 00000000 |

222.10.1.0 /30: Class C network, 24 network bits. 30 – 24 = 6 subnet bits. 2 to the 6th power = 64 valid subnets.

| NW Mask | 11111111 | 11111111 | 11111111 | 00000000 |
| SN Mask | 11111111 | 11111111 | 11111111 | **111111**00 |

145.45.0.0 /25: Class B network, 16 network bits. 25 – 16 = 9 subnet bits. 2 to the 9th power = 512 valid subnets.

| NW Mask | 11111111 | 11111111 | 00000000 | 00000000 |
| SN Mask | 11111111 | 11111111 | **11111111** | **1**0000000 |

20.0.0.0 255.192.0.0: Class A network with 8 network bits. Subnet mask converts to /10. 10 – 8 = 2 subnet bits.   2 to the 2nd power = 4 valid subnets.

| NW Mask | 11111111 | 00000000 | 00000000 | 00000000 |
| SN Mask | 11111111 | **11**000000 | 00000000 | 00000000 |

130.30.0.0 255.255.224.0:   Class B network with 16 network bits.   Subnet mask converts to /19 in prefix notation. 19 – 16 = 3 subnet bits. 2 to the 3rd power = 8 valid subnets.

| NW Mask | 11111111 | 11111111 | 00000000 | 00000000 |
| SN Mask | 11111111 | 11111111 | **111**00000 | 00000000 |

In the next chapter, we'll get even more work in with this vital skill using subnets with dotted decimal and prefix notation masks.   Let's have at it!

Studying for your CCENT or CCNA, or need to learn more about Cisco access lists? Visit my website for a totally free course on ACLs – offered to you in both video and text format! They're both packed with real-world labs designed to help you master ACLs.

ACL Video Boot Camp:

http://bit.ly/FreeACLCourse

ACL Text Course:

http://bit.ly/FreeCCNATutorials

CHAPTER 7:

"Number of Valid Subnets" Exercises

How many valid subnets are on each of these networks?
- 12.0.0.0 255.255.240.0
- 129.7.0.0 255.255.192.0
- 212.1.17.0 255.255.255.192
- 25.0.0.0 255.248.0.0
- 131.4.0.0 255.255.224.0

12.0.0.0 255.255.240.0:

This Class A network has 8 network bits in its mask. The subnet mask is 20 bits in length. 20 – 8 = 12 subnet bits.   2 to the 12th power = 4096 valid subnets.

129.7.0.0 255.255.192.0:

This Class B network has 16 network bits in its mask. The subnet mask is 18 bits long. 18 – 16 = 2 subnet bits. 2 to the 2nd power = 4 valid subnets.

212.1.17.0 255.255.255.192:

The Class C network mask is 24 bits. This subnet mask is 26 bits.   26 – 24 = 2 subnet bits. 2 to the 2nd power = 4 valid subnets.

25.0.0.0 255.248.0.0:

The Class A network mask is 8 bits. 255.248.0.0 is 13 bits. 13 – 8 = 5 subnet bits. 2 to the 5th power = 32 valid subnets.

131.4.0.0 255.255.224.0:

The Class B network mask is 16 bits. 255.255.224.0 is 19 bits. 19 – 16 = 3 subnet bits. 2 to the 3rd power = 8 valid subnets.

Great work!   Now do the same with these five networks:
- 213.1.17.0 255.255.255.192
- 137.9.0.0 255.255.240.0
- 214.8.9.0 255.255.255.240
- 142.3.0.0 255.255.254.0
- 32.0.0.0 255.254.0.0

213.1.17.0 255.255.255.192:

The Class C network mask is 24 bits. This subnet mask is 26 bits. 26 – 24 = 2 subnet bits. 2 to the 2nd power = 4 valid subnets.

137.9.0.0 255.255.240.0:

The Class B network mask is 16 bits. This subnet mask is 20 bits. 20 – 16 = 4 subnet bits. 2 to the 4th power = 16 valid subnets.

214.8.9.0 255.255.255.240:

The Class C network mask is 24 bits.   This subnet mask is 28 bits. 28 – 24 = 4 subnet bits. 2 to the 4th power = 16 valid subnets.

142.3.0.0 255.255.254.0:

The Class B network mask is 16 bits. This subnet mask is 23 bits.   23 – 16 = 7 subnet bits. 2 to the 7th power = 128 valid subnets.

32.0.0.0 255.254.0.0:

The Class A network mask is 8 bits. This subnet mask is 15 bits.   15 – 8 = 7 subnet bits.   2 to the 7th power = 128 valid subnets.

Let's do five more!
- 57.0.0.0 255.255.192.0
- 149.9.0.0 255.255.255.128
- 220.20.240.0 255.255.255.248
- 156.3.0.0 255.255.255.192
- 17.0.0.0 255.255.224.0

57.0.0.0 255.255.192.0:

The Class A network mask is 8 bits. This subnet mask is 18 bits.   18 – 8 = 10 subnet bits.   2 to the 10th power = 1024 valid subnets.

149.9.0.0 255.255.255.128:

The Class B network mask is 16 bits. This subnet mask is 25 bits. 25 − 16 = 9 subnet bits. 2 to the 9th power = 512 valid subnets.

220.20.240.0 255.255.255.248:

The Class C network mask is 24 bits. This subnet mask is 29 bits. 29 − 24 = 5 subnet bits. 2 to the 5th power = 32 valid subnets.

156.3.0.0 255.255.255.192:

The Class B network mask is 16 bits. This subnet mask is 26 bits. 26 − 16 = 10 subnet bits. 2 to the 10th power = 1024 valid subnets.

17.0.0.0 255.255.224.0:

The Class A network mask is 8 bits. This subnet mask is 19 bits. 19 − 8 = 11 subnet bits. 2 to the 11th power = 2048 valid subnets.

Five more with dotted decimal masks and then we'll change things up a bit.
- 23.0.0.0 255.192.0.0
- 171.3.0.0 255.255.248.0
- 209.2.7.0 255.255.255.240
- 217.2.3.0 255.255.255.252
- 37.0.0.0 255.224.0.0

23.0.0.0 255.192.0.0:

The Class A network mask is 8 bits. This subnet mask is 10 bits. 10 − 8 = 2 subnet bits. 2 to the 2nd power = 4 valid subnets.

171.3.0.0 255.255.248.0:

Our Class B network mask is 16 bits, and this subnet mask is 21 bits. 21 − 16 = 5 subnet bits. 2 to the 5th power = 32 valid subnets.

209.2.7.0 255.255.255.240:

Our Class C network mask is 24 bits, and this subnet mask is 28 bits. 28 − 24 = 4 subnet bits. 2 to the 4th power = 16 valid subnets.

217.2.3.0 255.255.255.252:

The Class C network mask is 24 bits, and this subnet mask is 30 bits. 30 − 24 = 6 subnet bits. 2 to the 6th power = 64 valid subnets.

37.0.0.0 255.224.0.0:

The Class A network mask is 8 bits in length, and this subnet mask is 11 bits. 11 − 8 = 3 subnet bits. 2 to the 3rd power = 8 valid subnets.

Let's get some work in with valid subnet calculations using masks expressed in prefix notation.

- 10.0.0.0 /19
- 136.1.0.0 /19
- 200.1.1.0 /26
- 210.10.10.0 / 27
- 140.7.0.0 /22

10.0.0.0 /19:

This Class A network has a network mask of /8. 19 − 8 = 11 subnet bits; 2 to the 11th power equals 2048 valid subnets.

136.1.0.0 /19:

This Class B network has a network mask of /16. 19 − 16 = 3 subnet bits. 2 to the 3rd power = 8 valid subnets.

200.1.1.0 /26:

This Class C network has a network mask of /24. 26 − 24 = 2 subnet bits. 2 to the 2nd power = 4 valid subnets.

210.10.10.0 /27:

This Class C network has a network mask of /24. 27 − 24 = 3 subnet bits. 2 to the 3rd power = 8 valid subnets.

140.7.0.0 /22:

This Class B network has a network mask of /16. 22 = 16 = 6 subnet bits. 2 to the 6th power = 64 valid subnets.

Five more and we're done!

- 156.4.0.0 /24
- 26.0.0.0 /13
- 25.0.0.0 /17
- 212.17.11.0 /28
- 166.6.0.0 /26

156.4.0.0 /24:

This Class B network has a network mask of /16. 24 – 16 = 8 subnet bits. 2 to the 8th power = 256 valid subnets.

26.0.0.0 /13:

This Class A network has a network mask of /8. 13 – 8 = 5 subnet bits. 2 to the 5th power = 32 valid subnets.

25.0.0.0 /17:

This Class A network has a network mask of /8. 17 – 8 = 9 subnet bits. 2 to the 9th power = 512 valid subnets.

212.17.11.0 /28:

This Class C network has a network mask of /24. 28 – 24 = 4 subnet bits. 2 to the 4th power equals 16 valid subnets.

166.6.0.0 /26:

This Class B network has a network mask of /16. 26 – 16 = 10 subnet bits. 2 to the 10th power equals 1024 valid subnets.

Whew! I know that was a lot of valid subnet calculations, but repetition with all of these skills is the key to them being automatic to you on an exam or job interview.

Now we're going to determine the number of valid host addresses on each of our subnets – and you're going to find the calculation there to be *very* familiar.

CHAPTER 8:

Determining The Number Of Valid Hosts On A Subnet

As with our "valid subnets" determination, the actual subnetting has already been done, and we need to come up with a value regarding that subnetting. In this case, it's the number of valid hosts on each subnet. We start by arriving at the number of host bits, and that's a quick trip:

32 – (the number of ones in the subnet mask) = # of host bits

Now that we have the number of host bits, what do we do with it, you ask? We plug it into this formula, even handier and dandier than the one you learned in the last section:

(2 to the power of the number of host bits) – 2 = # of valid host addresses on the subnet

Overall, it's a simple three-step process. Let's walk through an example using the network 200.10.10.0 /26.

1. 32 – 26 = 6 host bits.

2. 2 to the 6th power (2 x 2 x 2 x 2 x 2 x 2) is 64.

3. 64 – 2 = 62 valid hosts per subnet on 200.10.10.0 /26.

Done and *done!*

Let me point out two major differences between this determination and coming up with the number of valid *subnets* on a network.

- Determining the number of valid hosts uses the number of host bits, where determining the number of valid subnets uses the number of subnet bits. (Makes sense!)

- You only subtract the 2 in the "valid hosts" calculation.

Why subtract the two?   There are two addresses in each subnet that are considered unusable by hosts:

- The first address in the subnet, which is the subnet number itself.

- The last address in the subnet, which is the broadcast address for that subnet.

This concept will become clearer later in this book when we're calculating the actual range of valid IP addresses in a given subnet, along with the broadcast address for that subnet.   Be sure to subtract that two when calculating the number of valid hosts, especially on your exam – not to mention these practice questions.

Speaking of practice questions…how many valid hosts exist on each of *these* subnets?

- 220.11.10.0 /26
- 129.15.0.0 /21
- 222.22.2.0 /30
- 14.0.0.0 /20
- 221.10.78.0 255.255.255.224
- 143.34.0.0 255.255.255.192

The calculations:

220.11.10.0 /26: 32 – 26 = 6 host bits. 2 to the 6th power equals 64; subtract the two, and you have 62 valid host addresses on this subnet.

129.15.0.0 /21: 32 – 21 = 11 host bits. 2 to the 11th power equals 2048. Subtract your two unusable addresses, and you have 2046 valid hosts on this subnet.

222.22.2.0 /30: 32 – 30 = 2 host bits. 2 to the 2nd power equals 4. Subtract your two, and you have 2 valid host addresses on this subnet.

14.0.0.0 /20: 32 – 20 = 12 host bits.   2 to the 12th power equals 4096; subtract the two, and you have 4094 valid hosts on this subnet.

221.10.78.0 255.255.255.224: This mask converts to /27. 32 – 27 = 5 host bits. 2 to the 5th power = 32; 32 – 2 = 30 valid host addresses on this subnet.

143.34.0.0 255.255.255.192: This mask converts to /26. 32 – 26 = 6 host bits. 2 to the 6th power = 64; 64 – 2 = 62 valid host addresses on this subnet.

Coming up: More work with this particular calculation, and then I'll show you a lightning-fast method of taking an IP address and determining what subnet it's on. You'll find that to be a very helpful skill on certification exams and in real-world networking.

CHAPTER 9:

"Number Of Valid Hosts Per Subnet" Exercises

We'll start with some drills using masks in prefix notation and follow that with more work using dotted decimal masks. Let's start with these ten addresses:

- 11.0.0.0 /24
- 128.1.1.0 /20
- 23.0.0.0 /27
- 217.3.4.0 /29
- 132.2.0.0 /21
- 42.0.0.0 /20
- 147.4.0.0 /22
- 158.17.0.0 /29
- 211.3.9.0 / 28
- 205.42.83.0 /27

The calculations:

11.0.0.0 /24:
32 – 24 = 8 host bits. 2 to the 8th power = 256, and 256 – 2 invalid addresses equals 254 valid addresses per subnet.

128.1.1.0 /20:
32 – 20 = 12 host bits. (2 to the 12th power) – 2 = 4094 valid addresses per subnet.

23.0.0.0 /27:
32 – 27 = 5 host bits. (2 to the 5th power) – 2 = 30 valid addresses per subnet.

217.3.4.0 /29:
32 – 29 = 3 host bits. (2 to the 3rd power) – 2 = 6 valid addresses per subnet.

132.2.0.0 /21:
32 – 21 = 11 host bits. (2 to the 11th power) – 2 = 2046 valid addresses per subnet.

42.0.0.0 /20:
32 – 20 = 12 host bits. (2 to the 12th power) – 2 = 4094 valid addresses per subnet.

147.4.0.0 /22:
32 – 22 = 10 host bits. (2 to the 10th power) – 2 = 1022 valid addresses per subnet.

158.17.0.0 /29:
32 – 29 = 3 host bits. (2 to the 3rd power) – 2 = 6 valid addresses per subnet.

211.3.9.0 / 28:
32 – 28 = 4 host bits. (2 to the 4th power) - 2 = 14 valid addresses per subnet.

205.42.83.0 /27:
32 – 27 = 5 host bits. (2 to the 5th power) – 2 = 30 valid addresses per subnet.

Here's another batch of subnets to practice with:
- 59.0.0.0 /21
- 162.14.0.0 / 24
- 223.7.3.0 /25
- 172.3.0.0 /28
- 71.0.0.0 /22
- 222.4.10.0 /26
- 181.1.0.0 /27
- 78.0.0.0 /23
- 85.0.0.0 /25
- 92.0.0.0 /30

The calculations:

59.0.0.0 /21:
32 − 21 = 11 host bits. (2 to the 11th power) − 2 = 2046 valid addresses per subnet.

162.14.0.0 / 24:
32 − 24 = 8 host bits. (2 to the 8th power) − 2 = 254 valid addresses per subnet.

223.7.3.0 /25:
32 − 25 = 7 host bits. (2 to the 7th power) − 2 = 126 valid addresses per subnet.

172.3.0.0 /28:
32 − 28 = 4 host bits. (2 to the 4th power) − 2 = 14 valid addresses per subnet.

71.0.0.0 /22:
32 − 22 = 10 host bits. (2 to the 10th power) − 2 = 1022 valid addresses per subnet.

222.4.10.0 /26:
32 − 26 = 6 host bits. (2 to the 6th power) − 2 = 62 valid addresses per subnet.

181.1.0.0 /27:
32 − 27 = 5 host bits. (2 to the 5th power) − 2 = 30 valid addresses per subnet.

78.0.0.0 /23:
32 − 23 = 9 host bits. (2 to the 9th power) − 2 = 510 valid addresses per subnet.

85.0.0.0 /25:
32 − 25 = 7 host bits. (2 to the 7th power) − 2 = 126 valid addresses per subnet.

92.0.0.0 /30:
32 − 30 = 2 host bits. (2 to the 2nd power) − 2 = 2 valid addresses per subnet.

Great work! Let's practice this skill using masks in dotted decimal format.
- 199.7.3.0 255.255.255.128
- 188.83.0.0 255.255.255.0
- 128.3.0.0 255.255.240.0
- 197.32.48.0 255.255.255.240
- 99.0.0.0 255.255.252.0
- 111.0.0.0 255.255.248.0
- 155.55.0.0 255.255.255.248
- 144.132.0.0 255.255.255.252
- 195.7.100.0 255.255.255.192
- 75.0.0.0 255.255.255.224

The calculations:

199.7.3.0 255.255.255.128:
This mask begins with 25 ones (/25 in prefix notation). $32 - 25 = 7$ host bits. 2 to the 7th power = 128, and $128 - 2$ invalid addresses gives us 126 valid addresses per subnet.

188.83.0.0 255.255.255.0:
This mask is /24. $32 - 24 = 8$ host bits. 2 to the 8th power = 256. $256 - 2$ invalid addresses = 254 valid addresses per subnet.

128.3.0.0 255.255.240.0:
This mask is /20. $32 - 20 = 12$ host bits. 2 to the 12th power = 4096. Subtract the two invalid addresses and you have 4094 valid addresses per subnet.

197.32.48.0 255.255.255.240:
This mask has its first 28 bits set to one. $32 - 28 = 4$ host bits. 2 to the 4th power = 16. $16 - 2 = 14$ valid addresses per subnet.

99.0.0.0 255.255.252.0:
This mask has its first 22 bits set to one. $32 - 22 = 10$ host bits. 2 to the 10th power = 1024. $1024 - 2 = 1022$ valid addresses per subnet.

111.0.0.0 255.255.248.0:
This mask has its first 21 bits set to one. 32 – 21 = 11 host bits. 2 to the 11th power equals 2048. 2048 – 2 = 2046 valid addresses per subnet.

155.55.0.0 255.255.255.248:
This mask has its first 29 bits set to one. 32 – 29 = 3 host bits. 2 to the 3rd power = 8. 8 – 2 = 6 valid addresses per subnet.

144.132.0.0 255.255.255.252:
In prefix notation, this mask is /30. 32 – 30 = 2 host bits. 2 to the 2nd power = 4. 4 – 2 = 2 valid addresses per subnet.

195.7.100.0 255.255.255.192:
In prefix notation, this mask is /26. 32 – 26 = 6 host bits. 2 to the 6th power = 64. 64 – 2 = 62 valid addresses per subnet.

75.0.0.0 255.255.255.224:
In prefix notation, this mask is /27. 32 – 27 = 5 host bits. 2 to the 5th power = 32. Subtract the two and you have 30 valid addresses per subnet.

Let's get ten more done!
- 87.0.0.0 255.255.254.0
- 189.83.0.0 255.255.255.0
- 222.23.4.0 255.255.255.240
- 130.4.0.0 255.255.240.0
- 141.3.0.0 255.255.248.0
- 210.4.3.0 255.255.255.192
- 189.83.0.0 255.255.255.0
- 223.17.3.0 255.255.255.248
- 194.3.200.0 255.255.255.252
- 48.0.0.0 255.255.255.128

The calculations:

87.0.0.0 255.255.254.0:
The mask is /23. 32 – 23 = 9 host bits. 2 to the 9th power = 512. Subtract the two invalid addresses and you have 510 valid addresses per subnet.

189.83.0.0 255.255.255.0:
The mask is /24. 32 – 24 = 8 host bits. 2 to the 8th power = 256. Subtract the two invalid addresses and you have 254 valid addresses per subnet.

222.23.4.0 255.255.255.240:
This mask is /28. 32 – 28 = 4 host bits. 2 to the 4th power = 16. 16 – 2 = 14 valid addresses per subnet.

130.4.0.0 255.255.240.0:
The mask is /20. 32 – 20 = 12. 2 to the 12th power = 4096. Take off the two and you have 4094 valid addresses per subnet.

141.3.0.0 255.255.248.0:
The mask is /21. 32 – 21 = 11. 2 to the 11th power = 2048. Take off the two and you have 2046 valid addresses per subnet.

210.4.3.0 255.255.255.192:
The mask is /26. 32 – 26 = 6 host bits. 2 to the 6th power = 64; take off the two and you have 62 valid addresses per subnet.

189.83.0.0 255.255.255.0:
The mask is /24. 32 – 24 = 8 host bits. 2 to the 8th power = 256; remove the two and you have 254 valid addresses per subnet.
223.17.3.0 255.255.255.248:
The mask is /29. 32 – 29 = 3 host bits. 2 to the 3rd power = 8. Take the two off and you have six valid addresses per subnet.

194.3.200.0 255.255.255.252:

The mask is /30, and this mask leaves only 2 host bits (32 – 30 = 2). 2 to the 2nd power = 4; take the two off and you have two valid addresses per subnet.

48.0.0.0 255.255.255.128:

The mask is /25. 32 – 25 = 7 host bits. 2 to the 7th power gives us 128, and after subtracting the two naughty addresses, we have 126 valid addresses remaining.

Now we're going to apply our binary skills to an important subnet troubleshooting skill – determining *exactly* what subnet a particular IP address is residing on.

For more subnetting practice you can use anywhere, check out my Subnetting Success Practice Exam pack on Udemy. Over 170 additional questions, presented to you in practice exam format. Click that link and see for yourself (you also get the lowest price possible when you use this link!)

http://bit.ly/SubnetSuccess

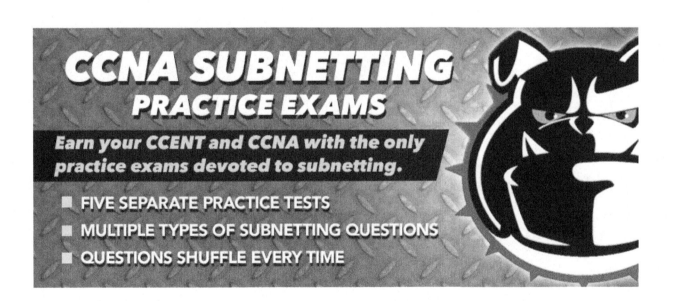

CHAPTER 10:

Determining The Subnet Of An IP Address

You'll find this to be a handy skill for passing your exams *and* troubleshooting real-world networks. If a host is on a different subnet than the subnet the admin *thinks* that host is on, IP connectivity issues can result. Sometimes it's easy to look at an address and mask and see which subnet it's on, and sometimes it's not quite as easy.

We'll take a longer look at the first example, and then I'll show you a method that'll allow you to determine an IP address's subnet in less than a minute.

To determine which subnet contains 10.17.2.14 /18, follow this simple three-step process:

1. Convert the IP address to a binary string.

2. Add up the part of the address covered by network *and* subnet bits.

3. Enjoy your victory. This step is optional but *highly* recommended.

Let's line up 10.17.2.14 with its subnet mask of /18.

	1st Octet	2nd Octet	3rd Octet	4th Octet
10.17.2.14	**00001010**	**00010001**	**00**000010	00001110
255.255.192.0	**11111111**	**11111111**	**11**000000	00000000

Adding up the first 18 bits in the binary string gives us 10.17.0.0, and that's our subnet – as long as you include the subnet mask. Both 10.17.0.0 /18 and 10.17.0.0 255.255.192.0 are acceptable ways to express the answer. Simply giving the network number isn't enough – you gotta include the mask.

Now that you know exactly what's going on at the bit level, let me show you the lightning-fast way to make this determination. You don't have to convert the entire IP address to find out the subnet. Just perform the decimal-to-binary conversion until you reach the number of bits indicated by the subnet mask. Let's tackle this question using the faster method.

"What subnet contains the IP address 217.17.23.200 /27?"

Convert the first 27 bits of that address to binary, and you have your answer:

11011001 00010001   00010111 110xxxxx

Convert that string back to dotted decimal, include the mask, and you're done. Both 217.17.23.192 /27 and 217.17.23.192 255.255.255.224 are acceptable ways to express the answer.

Let's tackle one more:

"What subnet contains the IP address 190.23.69.175 /22?"

Convert the address to binary, add up the first 22 bits, and you're done!   (You could also stop converting at the 22nd bit and add up what you have, as I"ve done here.)

190.23.69.175 =   10111110 00010111 010001xx   xxxxxxxx

The result: 190.23.68.0 /22 or 190.23.68.0 255.255.252.0.   Nothing to it, my friend!

Let's get a little more practice in with subnet determination. In the answers, I'll show you the full binary string, but feel free to just convert the number of bits indicated by the subnet mask to get the answer.

Tell me what subnet each of the following five addresses is on:

- 210.17.23.200 /27
- 24.194.34.12 /10
- 111.11.126.5 255.255.192.0
- 210.12.23.45 255.255.255.248
- 222.22.11.199 /28

And the subnets are...

210.17.23.200 /27: The full address in binary is **11010010 00010001 00010111 110**01000. Add the 27 bolded bits, and you have the subnet 210.17.23.192 /27.

24.194.34.12 /10: The full binary string is **00011000 11**000010 00100010 00001100. Convert the first ten bits back to decimal, and you have 24.192.0.0 /10.

111.11.126.5 255.255.192.0: The mask converts to /18. The binary string is **01101111 00001011 01**111110 00000101. Convert the first 18 bits back to decimal, and you have 111.11.64.0 /18.

210.12.23.45 255.255.255.248: The mask converts to /29. The full binary string is **11010010 00001100 00010111 00101**101. The first 29 bits reveal the subnet, 210.12.23.40 255.255.255.248.

222.22.11.199 /28: The full binary string is **11011110 00010110 00001011 1100**0111. The first 28 bits give us the subnet 222.22.11.192 /28.

More work with IP address / subnet determination in the next chapter!

http://bit.ly/SubnetSuccess

CHAPTER 11:

IP Address Subnet Exercises

A quick review of the three-step success process:

1. Convert the IP address to a binary string.

2. Add up the part of the address identified by a "1" in the network bits and subnet bits.

3. Enjoy your success.

If you want the conversion to be even faster, just do the IP address conversion out to the end of the subnet mask, and add up what you converted. For instance, if given the address 10.200.3.200 /12, there's no need to write out all 32 bits of the address (unless you want the practice!). Just write the first 12 out, and you're all set. In this case, the subnet is 10.192.0.0 /12.

	1st Octet	2nd Octet	3rd Octet	4th Octet
10.200.3.200 /12	00001010	1100xxxx	xxxxxxxx	xxxxxxxx

Let's get some work in with these addresses and determine what subnet they're on. In the answer section, I'll show the address converted to the point the mask ends.

- 46.37.2.14 /14
- 128.63.244.17 /19
- 211.134.13.200 /27
- 57.39.84.119 /18
- 144.83.22.53 /29
- 142.85.124.188 /20
- 189.187.181.146 /29
- 132.40.30.10 /20
- 111.44.160.217 /17
- 190.83.32.177 /27

The calculations:

46.37.2.14 /14 is on the 46.36.0.0 /14 subnet.

	1st Octet	2nd Octet	3rd Octet	4th Octet
46.37.2.14 /14	00101110	001001xx	xxxxxxxx	xxxxxxxx

128.63.244.17 /19 is on the 128.63.224.0 /19 subnet.

	1st Octet	2nd Octet	3rd Octet	4th Octet
128.63.244.17 /19	10000000	00111111	111xxxxx	xxxxxxxx

211.134.13.200 /27 is on the 211.134.13.192 /27 subnet.

	1st Octet	2nd Octet	3rd Octet	4th Octet
211.134.13.200 /27	11010011	10000110	00001101	110xxxxx

57.39.84.119 /18 is on the 57.39.64.0 /18 subnet.

	1st Octet	2nd Octet	3rd Octet	4th Octet
57.39.84.119 /18	00111001	00100111	01xxxxxx	xxxxxxxx

144.83.22.53 /29 is on the 144.83.22.48 /29 subnet.

	1st Octet	2nd Octet	3rd Octet	4th Octet
144.83.22.53 /29	10010000	01010011	00010110	00110xxx

142.85.124.188 /20 is on the 142.85.112.0 /20 network.

	1st Octet	2nd Octet	3rd Octet	4th Octet
142.85.124.188 /20	10001110	01010101	0111xxxx	xxxxxxxx

189.187.181.146 /29 is on the 189.187.181.144 /29 subnet.

	1st Octet	2nd Octet	3rd Octet	4th Octet
189.187.181.146 /29	10111101	10111011	10110101	10010xxx

132.40.30.10 /20 is on the 132.40.16.0 /20 subnet.

	1st Octet	2nd Octet	3rd Octet	4th Octet
132.40.30.10 /20	10000100	00101000	0001xxxx	xxxxxxxx

111.44.160.217 /17 is on the 111.44.128.0 /17 subnet.

	1st Octet	2nd Octet	3rd Octet	4th Octet
111.44.160.217 /17	01101111	00101100	1xxxxxxx	xxxxxxxx

190.83.32.177 /27 is on the 190.83.32.160 /27 subnet.

	1st Octet	2nd Octet	3rd Octet	4th Octet
190.83.32.177 /27	10111110	01010011	00100000	101xxxxx

Let's do five more, this time with dotted decimal masks.

- 89.23.48.211 255.255.255.128
- 221.17.211.53 255.255.255.192
- 200.83.24.216 255.255.255.240
- 144.83.22.49 255.255.252.0
- 187.12.48.217 255.255.224.0

The calculations:

89.23.48.211 255.255.255.128 is on the 89.23.48.128 255.255.255.128 (/25) subnet.

	1st Octet	2nd Octet	3rd Octet	4th Octet
89.23.48.211 255.255.255.128	01011001	00010111	00110000	1xxxxxxx

221.17.211.53 255.255.255.192 is on the 221.17.211.0 255.255.255.192 (/26) subnet.

	1st Octet	2nd Octet	3rd Octet	4th Octet
221.17.211.53 255.255.255.192	11011101	00010001	11010011	00xxxxxx

200.83.24.216 255.255.255.240 is on the 200.83.24.208 255.255.255.240 (/28) subnet.

	1st Octet	2nd Octet	3rd Octet	4th Octet
200.83.24.216 255.255.255.240	11001000	01010011	00011000	1101xxxx

144.83.22.49 255.255.252.0 is on the 144.83.20.0 255.255.252.0 (/22) subnet.

	1st Octet	2nd Octet	3rd Octet	4th Octet
144.83.22.49 255.255.252.0	10010000	01010011	000101xx	xxxxxxxx

187.12.48.217 255.255.224.0 is on the 187.12.32.0 255.255.224.0 subnet (/19).

	1st Octet	2nd Octet	3rd Octet	4th Octet
187.12.48.217 255.255.224.0	10111011	00001100	001xxxxx	xxxxxxxx

Next up, you'll learn a skill that will give you two important pieces of information with just one quick calculation. Sounds good to me! Let's get to it!

CHAPTER 12:

Determining A Subnet's Broadcast Address and Range Of Valid Addresses

In this section, you get two important pieces of subnetting information for the low, low cost of one simple conversion! Let's start with this question...

"What is the range of valid IP addresses for the subnet 210.46.111.0 /25?"

We arrive at this range by converting the IP address to a binary string and then identifying the host bits. With a /25 subnet mask, we know the last 7 bits are the host bits.

	Octet 1	Octet 2	Octet 3	Octet 4
210.46.111.0 /25	11010010	00101110	01101111	0**0000000**

You've just determined the broadcast address *and* the range of valid IP addresses for this subnet. This quick conversion gives us three vital pieces of information:

1. The address with all zeros for the host bits is the subnet address itself. Sometimes called the "all-zeroes address," this is not a valid host address.

2. The address with all ones for host bits is the broadcast address for this subnet. Also known as the "all-ones address," this is *also* not a valid host address. The all-zeros and all-ones addresses are the reason we subtract 2 when determining the number of valid hosts on a subnet.

3. All addresses between the all-zeroes address and the all-ones address are valid host addresses for this subnet.

We know 210.46.111.0 /25 is the subnet number, but what's the broadcast address? Just change those host bits to ones, and you've got it:

	Octet 1	Octet 2	Octet 3	Octet 4
210.46.111.0 /25: Subnet address, all host bits set to zero.	11010010	00101110	01101111	0**0000000**
Broadcast address, all host bits set to one.	11010010	00101110	01101111	0**1111111**

The all-ones address is 210.46.111.127 /25. Every address between our all-zeroes and all-ones addresses, from 210.46.111.1 /25 through 210.46.111.126 /25, is a valid IP address for this subnet.

Let's tackle a question with a smaller subnet mask, resulting in more host bits: *"Determine the broadcast address and the range of valid IP addresses for the subnet 150.10.64.0 /18."*

The conversion, with host bits in bold:

	1st Octet	2nd Octet	3rd Octet	4th Octet
150.10.64.0 /18	10010110	00001010	01**000000**	**00000000**

What's the resulting address when all host bits are set to one?

	Octet 1	Octet 2	Octet 3	Octet 4
150.10.64.0 /18: Subnet address, all host bits set to zero.	10010110	00001010	01**000000**	**00000000**
Broadcast address, all host bits set to one.	10010110	00001010	01**111111**	**11111111**

The broadcast address for that subnet is 150.10.127.255 /18. If you thought the third octet of the address would be 63, that *is* the sum of the host bits in that octet set to 1, but note the "64" bit was set to 1 as well. Even though the "64" bit is not a host bit, you still include it in the sum when it's set to one.

The range of valid IP addresses for this subnet is 150.10.64.1 /18 through 150.10.127.254 /18.

Coming up next, we'll get some more practice in with determining our broadcast addresses and address ranges, and then we'll run scenarios where we get to do the actual subnetting from the very beginning.

If you're studying for the CCENT, CCNA or Network+ exams, you have to know TCP and UDP inside and out. Use this free tutorial series to do just that! (All pages are on my website, www.thebryantadvantage.com)

The Handshake: http://bit.ly/TCPUDP1

The Sequence Numbers: http://bit.ly/TCPUDP2

The Sliding Window: http://bit.ly/TCPUDP3

The Headers: http://bit.ly/TCPUDP4

CHAPTER 13:

Broadcast Number / Valid Address Range Exercises

Determine the broadcast address and the range of valid IP addresses for the following subnets.

Question Batch #1:

- 17.200.0.0 /18
- 23.21.4.128 /27
- 99.87.40.0 /23
- 77.32.89.160 /29
- 55.14.64.0 /19

Answer Batch #1:

17.200.0.0 /18:

	Octet 1	Octet 2	Octet 3	Octet 4
Subnet address, all host bits set to zero.	00010001	11001000	00**000000**	**00000000**
Broadcast address, all host bits set to one.	00010001	11001000	00**111111**	**11111111**

Subnet address: 17.200.0.0 /18

Range of valid addresses: 17.200.0.1 – 17.200.63.254 /18

Broadcast address: 17.200.63.255 /18

23.21.4.128 /27:

	Octet 1	Octet 2	Octet 3	Octet 4
Subnet address, all host bits set to zero.	00010111	00010101	00000100	100**00000**
Broadcast address, all host bits set to one.	00010111	00010101	00000100	100**11111**

Subnet address: 23.21.4.128 /27

Range of valid addresses: 23.21.4.129 – 23.21.4.158 /27

Broadcast address: 23.21.4.159 /27

99.87.40.0 /23

	Octet 1	Octet 2	Octet 3	Octet 4
Subnet address, all host bits set to zero.	01100011	01010111	0010100**0**	**00000000**
Broadcast address, all host bits set to one.	01100011	01010111	0010100**1**	**11111111**

Subnet address: 99.87.40.0 /23

Range of valid addresses: 99.87.40.1 – 99.87.41.254 /23

Broadcast address: 99.87.41.255 /23

77.32.89.160 /29:

	Octet 1	Octet 2	Octet 3	Octet 4
Subnet address, all host bits set to zero.	01001101	00100000	01011001	10100**000**
Broadcast address, all host bits set to one.	01001101	00100000	01011001	10100**111**

Subnet address: 77.32.89.160 /29

Range of valid addresses: 77.32.89.161 – 77.32.89.166 /29

Broadcast address: 77.32.89.167 /29

55.14.64.0 /19:

	Octet 1	Octet 2	Octet 3	Octet 4
Subnet address, all host bits set to zero.	00110111	00001110	010**00000**	**00000000**
Broadcast address, all host bits set to one.	00110111	00001110	010**11111**	**11111111**

Subnet address: 55.14.64.0 /19

Range of valid addresses: 55.14.64.1 – 55.14.95.254 /19

Broadcast address: 55.14.95.255 /19

Question Batch #2:

Identify the broadcast address and the range of valid addresses present on each of the following subnets.

- 142.17.38.0 /28
- 154.100.19.128 /29
- 171.13.18.192 /28
- 133.111.40.0   255.255.254.0
- 188.42.87.32   255.255.255.252

Answer Batch #2:

142.17.38.0 /28:

	Octet 1	Octet 2	Octet 3	Octet 4
Subnet address, all host bits set to zero.	10001110	00010001	00100110	0000**0000**
Broadcast address, all host bits set to one.	10001110	00010001	00100110	0000**1111**

Subnet address: 142.17.38.0 /28

Range of valid addresses: 142.17.38.1 – 142.17.38.14 /28

Broadcast address: 142.17.38.15 /28

154.100.19.128 /29:

	Octet 1	Octet 2	Octet 3	Octet 4
Subnet address, all host bits set to zero.	10011010	01100100	00010011	10000**000**
Broadcast address, all host bits set to one.	10011010	01100100	00010011	10000**111**

Subnet address: 154.100.19.128 /29

Range of valid addresses: 154.100.19.129 – 154.100.19.134 /29

Broadcast address: 154.100.19.135 /29

171.13.18.192 /28:

	Octet 1	Octet 2	Octet 3	Octet 4
Subnet address, all host bits set to zero.	10101011	00001101	00010010	1100**0000**
Broadcast Address, all host bits set to one.	10101011	00001101	00010010	1100**1111**

Subnet address: 171.13.18.192 /28

Range of valid addresses: 171.13.18.193 – 172.13.18.206 /28

Broadcast address: 172.13.18.207 /28

133.111.40.0 255.255.254.0:

	Octet 1	Octet 2	Octet 3	Octet 4
Subnet address, all host bits set to zero.	10000101	01101111	0010100**0**	**00000000**
Broadcast address, all host bits set to one.	10000101	01101111	0010100**1**	**11111111**

Subnet address: 133.111.40.0 255.255.254.0 (/23)

Range of valid addresses: 133.111.40.1 – 133.111.41.254 255.255.254.0

Broadcast address: 133.111.41.255 255.255.254.0

188.42.87.32 255.255.255.252:

	Octet 1	Octet 2	Octet 3	Octet 4
Subnet address, all host bits set to zero.	10111100	00101010	01010111	001000**00**
Broadcast address, all host bits set to one.	10111100	00101010	01010111	001000**11**

Subnet address: 188.42.87.32 255.255.255.252 (/30)

The two valid addresses: 188.42.87.33 255.255.255.252 and 188.42.87.34 255.255.255.252

Broadcast address: 188.42.87.35 255.255.255.252

Question Batch 3:

Identify the broadcast address and the range of valid addresses present on each of the following subnets.

- 47.39.0.0 /21
- 217.38.119.48 255.255.255.240
- 99.13.0.0 /18
- 143.214.80.0 /22
- 172.18.200.0 255.255.252.0

Answer Batch 3:

47.39.0.0 /21:

	Octet 1	Octet 2	Octet 3	Octet 4
Subnet address, all host bits set to zero.	00101111	00100111	00000**000**	**00000000**
Broadcast address, all host bits set to one.	00101111	00100111	00000**111**	**11111111**

Subnet address: 47.39.0.0 /21

Range of valid addresses: 47.39.0.1 – 47.39.7.254 /21

Broadcast address: 47.39.7.255 /21

217.38.119.48 255.255.255.240:

	Octet 1	Octet 2	Octet 3	Octet 4
Subnet address, all host bits set to zero.	11011001	00100110	01110111	0011**0000**
Broadcast address, all host bits set to one.	11011001	00100110	01110111	0011**1111**

Subnet address: 217.38.119.48 255.255.255.240 (/28)

Range of valid addresses: 217.38.119.49 – 217.38.119.62 255.255.255.240

Broadcast address: 217.38.119.63 255.255.255.240

99.13.0.0 /18:

	Octet 1	Octet 2	Octet 3	Octet 4
Subnet address, all host bits set to zero.	01100011	00001101	00**000000**	**00000000**
Broadcast address, all host bits set to one.	01100011	00001101	00**111111**	**11111111**

Subnet address: 99.13.0.0 /18

Range of valid addresses: 99.13.0.1 – 99.13.63.254 /18

Broadcast address: 99.13.63.255 /18

143.214.80.0 /22:

	Octet 1	Octet 2	Octet 3	Octet 4
Subnet address, all host bits set to zero.	10001111	11010110	010100**00**	**00000000**
Broadcast address, all host bits set to one.	10001111	11010110	010100**11**	**11111111**

Subnet address: 143.214.80.0 /22

Valid address range: 143.214.80.1 – 143.214.83.254 /22

Broadcast address: 143.214.83.255 /22

172.18.200.0 255.255.252.0:

	Octet 1	Octet 2	Octet 3	Octet 4
Subnet address, all host bits set to zero.	10101100	00010010	110010**00**	**00000000**
Broadcast address, all host bits set to one.	10101100	00010010	110010**11**	**11111111**

Subnet address: 172.18.200.0 255.255.252.0 (/22)

Valid address range: 172.18.200.1 – 172.18.203.254 255.255.252.0

Broadcast address: 172.18.203.255 255.255.252.0

Now that we've practiced every skill we'll need to check someone else's subnetting, it's time to do some of our own!

Earn your CCNA with my CCNA Video Boot Camp and develop important real-world networking skills at the same time. I've packed this course with labs that will prepare you for success in the exam room and in real-life networking situations.

On top of that, it's ten bucks – and I guarantee you it's the best 10 bucks you'll ever spend on your CCNA studies. All videos downloadable, and there's no time limit. Join today!

http://bit.ly/CCNA2019

CHAPTER 14:

Subnetting, Actually

We'll use several of the skills we've mastered to this point in tackling this real-world scenario. Our client has come to us with the following requirements:

1. Use network 150.50.0.0.
2. We need at least 200 subnets.
3. We want 120 – 150 hosts per subnet.

We know 150.50.0.0 is a Class B network, and Class B networks have a /16 mask. That leaves 16 host bits, and subnetting is simply the process of borrowing host bits.

	1st Octet	2nd Octet	3rd Octet	4th Octet
NW Bits	11111111	11111111		
Host Bits			00000000	00000000

When I'm taking an exam and dealing with a question like this, I like to use the marker and board provided (make sure your marker is good BEFORE you hit the start button on your exam!) and just start doubling the number 1 until I get to the desired number of subnets. This highly complex (not) operation looks like this...

2 4 8 16 32 64 128 256

... and since I wrote eight numbers before I passed 200, my subnet mask has eight bits.

	1st Octet	2nd Octet	3rd Octet	4th Octet
NW Bits	11111111	11111111		
Subnet Bits			11111111	
Host Bits				00000000

We are not done. Eight subnet bits gives us 256 valid subnets, but there was one other requirement, and that was that each subnet has between 120 – 150 hosts. We have eight host bits remaining, making the number of valid hosts (2 to the 8th power) – 2 = 254. That's too many to meet our requirements, so we need to borrow one more host bit.

	1st Octet	2nd Octet	3rd Octet	4th Octet
NW Bits	11111111	11111111		
Subnet Bits			11111111	1
Host Bits				0000000

Number of valid subnets: 2 to the 9th power = 512. *Requirement met.*

Number of valid hosts: (2 to the 7th power) – 2 = 126. *Requirement met.*

The winning mask: 255.255.255.128, also expressed as /25.

That's all there is to it, and on exam day, you won't have to write all of this out. You'll be so good at it that you only need to write out the host bits and then do the subnetting. Let's go through one more:

1. We'll use network 220.10.10.0.

2. The client wants a minimum of 25 subnets.

3. The client wants no more than six hosts per subnet.

This is a Class C network, giving us 24 network bits and 8 host bits. What's the minimum number of host bits we need to borrow that gives us at least 25 subnets? Just double 2 until you pass 25...

2   4   8   16   32

... and that gives us 5 subnet bits. That leaves 3 host bits, and how many hosts per subnet does that leave us? (2 to the 3rd power) – 2 = 6, which *just* meets the requirement.

	1st Octet	2nd Octet	3rd Octet	4th Octet
NW Bits	11111111	11111111	11111111	
Subnet Bits				11111
Host Bits				000

Our resulting mask is 255.255.255.248, or /29.

The following three sections are packed with scenarios just like these. After you're done with those, we'll move on to variable-length subnet masking (VLSM).

CHAPTER 15:

Subnetting Scenarios

Question 1:

You're subnetting the 150.50.0.0 network. We need at least 200 subnets. No mention has been made of the number of required hosts per subnet. What mask results when you borrow the minimum number of host bits needed to meet the subnet requirement?

This Class B network has 16 network bits and 16 host bits. As you know and as I'll (try not to) endlessly remind you, we always borrow host bits for subnetting.

	1st Octet	2nd Octet	3rd Octet	4th Octet
Network Bits	11111111	11111111		
Subnet Bits				
Host Bits			00000000	00000000

The number of subnets is (2 to the *n*th power), with *n* being the number of subnet bits. The fewest number of subnet bits that gives us at least 200 subnets is eight (2 to the 8th power = 256.) Borrowing eight host bits results in a subnet mask of 255.255.255.0, which is expressed in prefix notation as /24.

	1st Octet	2nd Octet	3rd Octet	4th Octet
Network Bits	11111111	11111111		
Subnet Bits			11111111	
Host Bits				00000000

Question 2:

In subnetting the 180.100.0.0 network, you need to create at least 300 subnets while allowing at least 60 host addresses per subnet. What mask meets the host address requirement while maximizing the number of available subnets?

We have a Class B network with a network mask of /16 and 16 host bits *ripe* for borrowing for subnetting.

	1st Octet	2nd Octet	3rd Octet	4th Octet
Network Bits	11111111	11111111		
Subnet Bits				
Host Bits			00000000	00000000

The phrase "maximizing the number of available subnets" means we want to borrow as many host bits as possible while leaving just enough host bits to give us at least 60 addresses per subnet.

The formula for "number of host addresses" is (2 to the nth power – 2), with n being the number of host bits. The lowest number that results in a value greater than 60 is six (2 to the 6th power – 2 = 62). That would leave ten bits for subnetting, giving us 1024 valid subnets, with 2 to the 10th power equaling 1024. The magic mask here is 255.255.255.192 (/26).

	1st Octet	2nd Octet	3rd Octet	4th Octet
Network Bits	11111111	11111111		
Subnet Bits			11111111	11
Host Bits				000000

Question 3:

You're subnetting the 240.17.39.0 network and your boss requests you come up with a mask that will give you at least 35 subnets to work with. What is the greatest number of hosts such a mask can result in?

This Class C network gives us eight host bits to work with for subnetting.

	1st Octet	2nd Octet	3rd Octet	4th Octet
Network Bits	11111111	11111111	11111111	
Subnet Bits				
Host Bits				00000000

For 35 subnets, we'd need to borrow at least six host bits (2 to the 6th power = 64). If we borrowed one less bit, we'd have only 32 valid subnets (2 to the 5th power = 32). Borrowing those six host bits leaves us only two host bits, which results in two valid addresses per subnet (2 to the 2nd power – 2) = 2. The resulting mask is 255.255.255.252 (/30).

	1st Octet	2nd Octet	3rd Octet	4th Octet
Network Bits	11111111	11111111	11111111	
Subnet Bits				111111
Host Bits				00

Question 4:

You're subnetting the 19.0.0.0 network and your supervisor requests you apply a subnet mask that results in over 3500 subnets and over 3500 valid addresses per subnet. Is this possible? If so, what mask or masks will make this happen?

Our Class A network has a whopping 24 host bits we can borrow for subnetting.

	1st Octet	2nd Octet	3rd Octet	4th Octet
Network Bits	11111111			
Subnet Bits				
Host Bits		00000000	00000000	00000000

The best approach is to figure out the minimum number of subnet bits we'll need for 3500+ subnets and then see if we have enough host bits left for the same minimum number of host addresses per subnet.

The lowest number of host bits we can borrow to end up with 3500+ subnets is 12, since 2 to the 12th power equals 4096. (11 subnet bits would give us 2048 subnets.)

After borrowing 12 host bits for subnetting, we have 12 host bits left. Luckily, that gives us 4094 host addresses (2 to the 12th power – 2 = 4094).

	1st Octet	2nd Octet	3rd Octet	4th Octet
Network Bits	11111111			
Subnet Bits		11111111	1111	
Host Bits			0000	00000000

This mask, 255.255.240.0 (/20), is the only mask that can meet both requirements. If we had borrowed one more subnet bit, we would have had only 11 left, and that wouldn't give us enough addresses per subnet.

Question 5:

You're assigned the 140.40.0.0 network to subnet. Your boss has asked you to come up with a mask that results in at least 500 subnets and at least 150 addresses per subnet. Is this possible? If so, what mask or masks will make this happen?

Since this is a Class B network, we have 16 host bits available for borrowing.

	1st Octet	2nd Octet	3rd Octet	4th Octet
Network Bits	11111111	11111111		
Subnet Bits				
Host Bits			00000000	00000000

The best approach is to figure out how many host bits we need to borrow for 500 subnets and go from there. We'd need at least nine subnet bits, since 2 to the 9th power = 512. Any fewer subnet bits and we don't have enough subnets for the requirement.

Borrowing those nine bits leaves us seven host bits...

	1st Octet	2nd Octet	3rd Octet	4th Octet
Network Bits	11111111	11111111		
Subnet Bits			11111111	1
Host Bits				0000000

… and that's not enough for 150 addresses per subnet. (2 to the 7th power – 2) = 126 valid addresses per subnet. The minimum amount of host bits we need for 150 addresses per subnet is eight. That would leave us only eight subnet bits, which isn't enough to meet the 500-subnet requirement. No subnet mask meets both requirements. If your boss doesn't believe you, buy him a copy of this book!

In return, he can pay for your very small tuition to my CCNA Video Boot Camp! :)

http://bit.ly/CCNA2019

CHAPTER 16:

Son Of Subnetting Situations

Question 1:

You're working with the 147.39.0.0 network. You need a mask that results in at least 120 subnets and between 200 - 300 valid addresses per subnet. What mask or masks will accomplish this?

This Class B network gives us 16 network bits and 16 host bits.

	1st Octet	2nd Octet	3rd Octet	4th Octet
Network Bits	11111111	11111111		
Subnet Bits				
Host Bits			00000000	00000000

The lowest number of subnet bits that gives us at least 120 subnets is seven. That results in 128 valid subnets (2 to the 7th power).

	1st Octet	2nd Octet	3rd Octet	4th Octet
Network Bits	11111111	11111111		
Subnet Bits			1111111	
Host Bits			0	00000000

The problem with that mask comes in with the number of host bits we still have. Those nine remaining host bits give us 510 valid host addresses per subnet (2 to the 9th power = 512 – 2 = 510), violating the requirement that we have between 200 and 300 valid addresses per subnet. We need to borrow at least one more host bit.

	1st Octet	2nd Octet	3rd Octet	4th Octet
Network Bits	11111111	11111111		
Subnet Bits			11111111	
Host Bits				00000000

Borrowing one more subnet bit gives us 256 valid subnets (2 to the 8th power) and 254 valid addresses per subnet (2 to the 8th power – 2). The mask 255.255.255.0 (/24) meets both requirements.

Question 2:

You're subnetting the 70.0.0.0 network. You need at least 1800 subnets for your network, and you want to maximize the number of valid addresses per subnet. What is the best mask for the job?

This Class A network gives us 8 network bits and 24 host bits.

	1st Octet	2nd Octet	3rd Octet	4th Octet
Network Bits	11111111			
Subnet Bits				
Host Bits		00000000	00000000	00000000

For 1800 subnets, you need a minimum of 11 subnet bits. 2 to the 11th power = 2048 subnets. Borrowing 11 bits gives us a mask of 255.255.224.0 (/19). This mask meets the "number of subnets" requirement while leaving the maximum number of host bits.

	1st Octet	2nd Octet	3rd Octet	4th Octet
Network Bits	11111111			
Subnet Bits		11111111	111	
Host Bits			00000	00000000

Question 3:

You're subnetting the 210.3.22.0 network. You need at least 10 valid subnets and at least 10 valid addresses on each of those subnets. Is this possible? If so, what mask or masks will meet both requirements?

This Class C network leaves us only eight host bits to borrow for subnetting. Let's see if that's enough.

	1st Octet	2nd Octet	3rd Octet	4th Octet
Network Bits	11111111	11111111	11111111	
Subnet Bits				
Host Bits				00000000

The minimum number of subnet bits that give us at least 10 valid subnets is four (2 to the 4th power = 16). That leaves us four host bits, which is enough to give us 14 valid hosts per subnet (2 to the 4th power – 2). The mask 255.255.255.240 (/28) is the only mask that meets both requirements. One subnet bit more or less and one of our requirements is violated.

	1st Octet	2nd Octet	3rd Octet	4th Octet
Network Bits	11111111	11111111	11111111	
Subnet Bits				1111
Host Bits				0000

Question 4:

You're subnetting the 150.5.0.0 network. You need at least 400 subnets, and no more than 100 valid host addresses should be on each subnet. What single mask will meet both requirements and maximize the number of host addresses per subnet?

This Class B network gives us 16 network bits and 16 host bits.

	1st Octet	2nd Octet	3rd Octet	4th Octet
Network Bits	11111111	11111111		
Subnet Bits				
Host Bits			00000000	00000000

We want as many host addresses per subnet as possible without going over 100. The number of host bits that meets that requirement is six (2 to the 6th power = 64 – 2 = 62). If we borrowed one more bit, that would put us over 100 host addresses per subnet (2 to the 7th power = 128 – 2 = 126).

That means we need to borrow 10 host bits for subnetting, which results in way more than 400 subnets -- 1024 of them, to be exact. The resulting mask is 255.255.255.192 (/26).

	1st Octet	2nd Octet	3rd Octet	4th Octet
Network Bits	11111111	11111111		
Subnet Bits			11111111	11
Host Bits				000000

Question 5:

You're subnetting the 30.0.0.0 network. You want to maximize the number of valid subnets while allowing for as many host addresses as possible without exceeding 1000 of them per subnet. What is the best mask for the job?

This Class A network gives us 8 network bits and 24 host bits to borrow for subnetting.

	1st Octet	2nd Octet	3rd Octet	4th Octet
Network Bits	11111111			
Subnet Bits				
Host Bits		00000000	00000000	00000000

To maximize the number of host addresses per subnet but not exceed 1000, we'll need nine host bits (2 to the 9th power − 2 = 510). If you have one more host bit, you'll have over 1000 hosts per subnet.

We have 24 bits, so if we want only nine host bits, we'll need to borrow a whopping 15 host bits for subnetting.

	1st Octet	2nd Octet	3rd Octet	4th Octet
Network Bits	11111111			
Subnet Bits		11111111	1111111	
Host Bits			0	00000000

The resulting mask is 255.255.254.0 (/23).

Coming up next – more subnetting!

http://bit.ly/SubnetSuccess

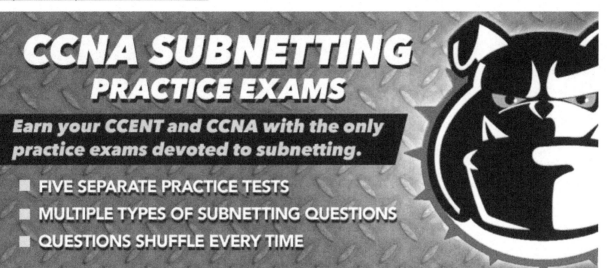

CHAPTER 17:

Subnetting Situations III

Question 1:

You're working with the 211.17.200.0 network. You want the total number of subnets to be as close as possible to the number of valid IP addresses per subnet. What's the best mask for the job?

Our Class C network gives us eight host bits to work with.

	1st Octet	2nd Octet	3rd Octet	4th Octet
Network Bits	11111111	11111111	11111111	
Subnet Bits				
Host Bits				00000000

In any situation where you want roughly the same number of subnets as you do valid addresses per subnet, just take half the host bits and borrow them for subnetting. That's true regardless of network class type. In this example, we'd borrow four of the available eight host bits.

	1st Octet	2nd Octet	3rd Octet	4th Octet
Network Bits	11111111	11111111	11111111	
Subnet Bits				1111
Host Bits				0000

That gives us a mask of 255.255.255.240 (/28), which gives us 16 valid subnets and 14 valid host addresses per subnet. (2 to the 4th power and 2 to the 4th power minus 2, respectively.)

Question 2:

In subnetting the 89.0.0.0 network, you want as many subnets as possible without exceeding 1000. There is no "number of hosts" requirement. What's the best mask for the job?

Our Class A network gives us 24 host bits to work with.

	1st Octet	2nd Octet	3rd Octet	4th Octet
Network Bits	11111111			
Subnet Bits				
Host Bits		00000000	00000000	00000000

To get as many subnets as we can without going over a thousand, we need to borrow nine subnet bits (2 to the 9th power = 512).

	1st Octet	2nd Octet	3rd Octet	4th Octet
Network Bits	11111111			
Subnet Bits		11111111	1	
Host Bits			0000000	00000000

The resulting subnet mask is 255.255.128.0 (/17).

Question 3:

You're subnetting the 101.0.0.0 network, and you need at least 1000 subnets while maximizing the number of valid host addresses per subnet. What mask will accomplish this?

Our Class A network gives us 24 host bits to work with.

	1st Octet	2nd Octet	3rd Octet	4th Octet
Network Bits	11111111			
Subnet Bits				
Host Bits		00000000	00000000	00000000

To meet both requirements, we need to borrow the absolute lowest number of host bits for subnetting while meeting the 1000-subnet requirement. This ensures the largest number of valid hosts per subnet.

The lowest number of subnet bits that gives us at least 1000 subnets is ten (2 to the 10th power = 1024). The resulting mask is 255.255.192.0 (/18).

	1st Octet	2nd Octet	3rd Octet	4th Octet
Network Bits	11111111			
Subnet Bits		11111111	11	
Host Bits			000000	00000000

Question 4:

You're working with the 199.14.130.0 network. You need at least 15 subnets and at least five valid addresses per subnet. What mask or masks will get this job done?

Our Class C network gives us eight host bits to work with.

	1st Octet	2nd Octet	3rd Octet	4th Octet
Network Bits	11111111	11111111	11111111	
Subnet Bits				
Host Bits				00000000

If we need at least 15 subnets (and we do), we need to borrow at least 4 host bits for subnetting, which results in 16 valid subnets (2 to the 4th power).

	1st Octet	2nd Octet	3rd Octet	4th Octet
Network Bits	11111111	11111111	11111111	
Subnet Bits				1111
Host Bits				0000

This 255.255.255.240 (/28) mask also results in 14 valid addresses per subnet (2 to the 4th power – 2), so this mask meets both requirements.

BUT – is that the only mask that will work? What if we borrow another host bit for subnetting?

	1st Octet	2nd Octet	3rd Octet	4th Octet
Network Bits	11111111	11111111	11111111	
Subnet Bits				11111
Host Bits				000

This 255.255.255.248 (/29) mask results in 32 valid subnets (2 to the 5th power) and 6 valid addresses per subnet (2 to the 3rd power – 2), so it also meets the requirements.

I have a pretty good idea that borrowing yet another host bit for subnetting will *not* meet both requirements, but let's have a look.

	1st Octet	2nd Octet	3rd Octet	4th Octet
Network Bits	11111111	11111111	11111111	
Subnet Bits				111111
Host Bits				00

No go! This 255.255.255.252 (/30) mask gives us plenty of subnets – 64 of them, to be exact – but results in only 2 valid host addresses per subnet.

The winning masks are 255.255.255.240 (/28) and 255.255.255.248 (/29).

Question 5:

In subnetting 170.17.0.0, you need at least 900 valid host addresses per subnet. You have no specific number of subnets in mind, but you want as many as you can get while meeting the requirement regarding host addresses. What mask is the best choice?

Our Class B network brings with it 16 host bits to borrow for subnetting.

	1st Octet	2nd Octet	3rd Octet	4th Octet
Network Bits	11111111	11111111		
Subnet Bits				
Host Bits			00000000	00000000

To allow at least 900 addresses per subnet *and* maximize the number of overall subnets, we need to borrow as many host bits for subnetting as we can while leaving enough host bits to meet that minimum.

We need at least 10 host bits (2 to the 10th power = 1024 – 2 = 1022) to reach the required minimum of 900 host addresses per subnet. With 16 host bits to begin with, borrowing six of them for subnetting will give us the maximum number of subnets while still meeting the host requirement.

	1st Octet	2nd Octet	3rd Octet	4th Octet
Network Bits	11111111	11111111		
Subnet Bits			111111	
Host Bits			00	00000000

The 255.255.252.0 (/22) mask is the best choice for this situation. It delivers 1022 valid addresses per subnet and 64 valid subnets. Had we borrowed one more host bit for subnetting, we would have had less than 900 valid addresses per subnet (510 of them, to be exact.)

Question 6:

You're subnetting the 150.4.0.0 network and want to have at least 380 hosts per subnet while maximizing the overall number of subnets. What's the best mask for the job?

This Class B network gives us 16 host bits to work with. The lowest number of host bits that will give us at least 380 hosts is nine (2 to the 9th power – 2 = 510). To maximize the number of subnets, we need to borrow enough host bits for subnetting to leave only those nine host bits.

We start with 16 host bits, so we need to borrow seven host bits for subnetting to end up with the desired nine host bits. The resulting mask is 255.255.254.0 (/23).

	1st Octet	2nd Octet	3rd Octet	4th Octet
Network Bits	11111111	11111111		
Subnet Bits			1111111	
Host Bits			0	00000000

Question 7:

You're subnetting the 214.13.8.0 network. You want to end up with at least 60 subnets while maximizing the number of hosts per subnet. What is the best mask to use in this situation?

This Class C network gives us eight host bits to work with. For a minimum of 60 subnets, we'll need to borrow six of those eight bits (2 to the 6th power = 64 valid subnets). That results in a subnet mask of 255.255.255.252 (/30), which leaves only two host bits and therefore two valid host addresses on this particular subnet (2 to the 2nd power – 2 = 2).

	1st Octet	2nd Octet	3rd Octet	4th Octet
Network Bits	11111111	11111111	11111111	
Subnet Bits				111111
Host Bits				00

Question 8:

In subnetting the 172.17.0.0 network, you want at least 300 subnets while ending up with at least 55 valid host addresses per subnet. What mask or masks will accomplish this?

We have 16 host bits to work with when dealing with a Class B network. The first number of subnet bits that gives us at least 300 subnets is nine (2 to the 9th power = 512). That leaves seven host bits, which results in 126 valid addresses per subnet (2 to the 7th power – 2 = 126). The resulting mask is 255.255.255.128 (/25).

	1st Octet	2nd Octet	3rd Octet	4th Octet
Network Bits	11111111	11111111		
Subnet Bits			11111111	1
Host Bits				0000000

Ten subnet bits will also give us over 300 subnets. We end up with 1024 of them (2 to the 10th power = 1024). The remaining six host bits result in 62 valid addresses per subnet (2 to the 6th power – 2 = 62). The resulting mask, 255.255.255.192 (/26), *also* meets the requirements.

	1st Octet	2nd Octet	3rd Octet	4th Octet
Network Bits	11111111			
Subnet Bits		11111111	11111111	11
Host Bits				000000

Eleven subnet bits results in over 2000 subnets (2 to the 11th power = 2048), but the remaining five host bits are not enough to meet the 55-hosts-per-subnet requirement (2 to the 5th power – 2 = 30 valid addresses per subnet.)   The 255.255.255.128 (/25) and 255.255.255.192 (/26) masks are the only ones that meet both requirements.

You've really done some great work here – particularly those of you totally new to subnetting. You've taken some fundamental conversion skills and put them to work in real-world subnetting situations. Congratulate yourself, take a little break, and then let's move forward to VLSM.

CHAPTER 18:

Variable-Length Subnet Masking (VLSM)

To this point with our subnetting, we've been slicing a pie of addresses into nice, neat even slices where every subnet has the same number of hosts and valid addresses. There will come a time, though, where you don't *want* the subnets to be the same size. Let's say you have a classic point-to-point network segment where you only need two addresses.

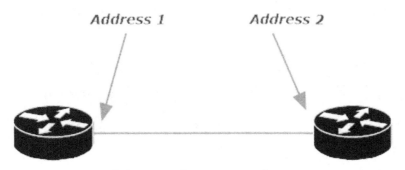

Point-to-Point Networks
Require Only 2 Addresses

If you use a subnet that contains 2000 valid addresses on that segment, you're wasting 1998 addresses. We're much better off slicing our "address pie" into uneven slices using variable-length subnet masking – VLSM.

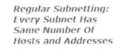

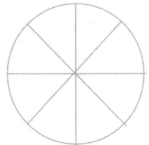

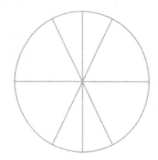

We're doing the same thing we did in our earlier subnetting exercises, but now we're tailoring it to more particular addressing requirements and saving addresses at the same time. You'll see exactly what I mean as we go through performing VLSM on the 150.50.0.0 network, where our subnets and their host requirements are as follows:

- Subnet A: 200 host addresses
- Subnet B: 50 host addresses
- Subnet C: 25 host addresses
- Subnet D: 5 host addresses
- Subnet E: 2 host addresses

As you proceed with a VLSM scheme, ask yourself one simple question: *"What subnet is created with the minimum required number of host bits set to zero?"*

Subnet A needs 200 host addresses, and performing the calculation we're very familiar with, we know we'll need eight host bits (2 to the 8th power = 256 – 2 = 254 hosts.) What subnet of 150.50.0.0 is created with all eight host bits set to zero?

	1st Octet	2nd Octet	3rd Octet	4th Octet
150.50.0.0	10010110	00110010	00000000	**00000000**
Mask With All Eight Host Bits Set To Zero	11111111	11111111	11111111	**00000000**

The mask is 255.255.255.0 (/24).

As you develop your VLSM scheme, it's a *fantastic* idea to keep a running chart of your scheme, including the subnet mask, the subnet number, and the broadcast address for that subnet. You know everything in between those two values is a valid host address, but I like to put a column for that in there as well.

Subnet Name	Subnet & Mask	Subnet Number	BC Address	Valid Host Range
Subnet A	150.50.0.0 /24	150.50.0.0 /24	150.50.0.255 /24	150.50.0.1 – 150.50.0.254 /24

Subnet B is up next, and we'll start that subnet with 150.50.1.0, the very next address up from Subnet A's broadcast address. We need at least 50 valid addresses on that subnet. Using the "valid hosts" calculation, we quickly realize we need six host bits (2 to the 6th power = 64 – 2 = 62 valid hosts on this subnet). What subnet of 150.50.1.0 is created with all six host bits set to zero?

	1st Octet	2nd Octet	3rd Octet	4th Octet
150.50.1.0	10010110	00110010	00000001	00**000000**
Mask With All Six Host Bits Set To Zero	11111111	11111111	11111111	11**000000**

Our mask is /26 (255.255.255.192). The resulting broadcast address and valid host range is…

	1st Octet	2nd Octet	3rd Octet	4th Octet
Subnet address, all host bits set to zero: 150.50.1.0 /26	10010110	00110010	00000001	00**000000**
Broadcast address, all host bits set to one: 150.50.1.63 /26	10010110	00110010	00000001	00**111111**

Let's update our VLSM chart and then take care of Subnet C.

Subnet Name	Subnet & Mask	Subnet Number	BC Address	Valid Host Range
Subnet A	150.50.0.0 /24	150.50.0.0 /24	150.50.0.255 /24	150.50.0.1 – 150.50.0.254 /24
Subnet B	150.50.1.0 /26	150.50.1.0 /26	150.50.1.63 /26	150.50.1.1 – 150.50.1.62 /26

We'll begin Subnet C with 150.50.1.64, the next address up from Subnet B's broadcast address. Subnet C's host requirement is 25, so we'll need five host bits (2 to the 5th power – 32 – 2 = 30 valid addresses). That means we have a subnet mask of /27, or 255.255.255.224.

	1st Octet	2nd Octet	3rd Octet	4th Octet
150.50.1.64	10010110	00110010	00000001	010**00000**
Mask With All Five Host Bits Set To Zero	11111111	11111111	11111111	111**00000**

The resulting broadcast address for Subnet C:

	1st Octet	2nd Octet	3rd Octet	4th Octet
Subnet address, all host bits set to zero: 150.50.1.64 /27	10010110	00110010	00000001	010**00000**
Broadcast address, all host bits set to one: 150.50.1.95 /27	10010110	00110010	00000001	010**11111**

Update the chart with Subnet C's information.

Subnet Name	Subnet & Mask	Subnet Number	BC Address	Valid Host Range
Subnet A	150.50.0.0 /24	150.50.0.0 /24	150.50.0.255 /24	150.50.0.1 – 150.50.0.254 /24
Subnet B	150.50.1.0 /26	150.50.1.0 /26	150.50.1.63 /26	150.50.1.1 – 150.50.1.62 /26
Subnet C	150.50.1.64 /27	150.50.1.64 /27	150.50.1.95 /27	150.50.1.65 – 150.50.1.94 /27

We move up one address from Subnet C's broadcast address to 150.50.1.96, where we'll begin Subnet D. That subnet needs only five host addresses, so we can get by with three host bits (2 to the 3rd power = 8 – 2 = 6 valid addresses). We'll apply a /29 mask to 150.50.1.96:

	1st Octet	2nd Octet	3rd Octet	4th Octet
150.50.1.96	10010110	00110010	00000001	01100**000**
Mask With All Three Host Bits Set To Zero	11111111	11111111	11111111	11111**000**

The result:

	1st Octet	2nd Octet	3rd Octet	4th Octet
Subnet address, all host bits set to zero: 150.50.1.96 /29	10010110	00110010	00000001	01100**000**
Broadcast address, all host bits set to one: 150.50.1.103 /29	10010110	00110010	00000001	01100**111**

The updated chart:

Subnet Name	Subnet & Mask	Subnet Number	BC Address	Valid Host Range
Subnet A	150.50.0.0 /24	150.50.0.0 /24	150.50.0.255 /24	150.50.0.1 – 150.50.0.254 /24
Subnet B	150.50.1.0 /26	150.50.1.0 /26	150.50.1.63 /26	150.50.1.1 – 150.50.1.62 /26
Subnet C	150.50.1.64 /27	150.50.1.64 /27	150.50.1.95 /27	150.50.1.65 – 150.50.1.94 /27
Subnet D	150.50.1.96 /29	150.50.1.96 /29	150.50.1.103 /29	150.50.1.97 – 150.50.1.102 /29

We'll start Subnet E on 150.50.1.104 and apply a /30 mask, leaving only two host addresses.

	1st Octet	2nd Octet	3rd Octet	4th Octet
150.50.1.104	10010110	00110010	00000001	011010**00**
Mask With 2 Host Bits Set To Zero	11111111	11111111	11111111	111111**00**

The result:

	1st Octet	2nd Octet	3rd Octet	4th Octet
Subnet address, all host bits set to zero: 150.50.1.104 /30	10010110	00110010	00000001	011010**00**
Broadcast address, all host bits set to one: 150.50.1.107 /30	10010110	00110010	00000001	011010**11**

Our final VLSM scheme:

Subnet Name	Subnet & Mask	Subnet Number	BC Address	Valid Host Range
Subnet A	150.50.0.0 /24	150.50.0.0 /24	150.50.0.255 /24	150.50.0.1 – 150.50.0.254 /24
Subnet B	150.50.1.0 /26	150.50.1.0 /26	150.50.1.63 /26	150.50.1.1 – 150.50.1.62 /26
Subnet C	150.50.1.64 /27	150.50.1.64 /27	150.50.1.95 /27	150.50.1.65 – 150.50.1.94 /27
Subnet D	150.50.1.96 /29	150.50.1.96 /29	150.50.1.103 /29	150.50.1.97 – 150.50.1.102 /29
Subnet E	150.50.1.104 /30	150.50.1.104 /30	150.50.1.107 /30	150.50.1.105 – 150.50.1.106 /30

In the next chapter, we'll get more work in with VLSM, and then it's time for some serious route summarization. Let's get it done!

CHAPTER 19:

VLSM Exercises

For each exercise, use the subnet mask that allows the minimum amount of host addresses while still meeting the requirements.

VLSM Exercise 1:

Given the 183.17.0.0 network, create VLSM subnets using these minimum host requirements:

- Subnet A, 290 hosts
- Subnet B, 211 hosts
- Subnet C, 78 hosts
- Subnet D, 39 hosts
- Subnet E, 4 hosts

With this Class B network, we have 16 network bits and 16 host bits. For Subnet A's 290 hosts, we'll need at least 9 of those host bits (2 to the 9th power = 512 – 2 = 510 valid host addresses.)

That leaves seven subnet bits, so our mask will be 255.255.254.0 (/23).

/23 mask	11111111	11111111	1111111**0**	**00000000**
All-zeroes address: 183.17.0.0 /23	10110111	00010001	0000000**0**	**00000000**
All-ones address: 183.17.1.255 /23	10110111	00010001	0000000**1**	**11111111**

The address with all host bits set to zero is the subnet address; the address with all host bits set to one is the broadcast address for that subnet. Everything between the two is the range of valid IP addresses for that subnet. I'm using a slightly different chart to keep up with our subnet address assignments than the one I used in the VLSM Theory chapter, leaving out the somewhat redundant "Subnet & Mask" column, which will always be the same as the subnet address itself.

	Subnet Address	Valid Addresses	Broadcast Add.
Subnet A	183.17.0.0 /23	183.17.0.1 – 183.17.1.254 /23	183.17.1.255 /23

So far, so good! The very next address up from that broadcast address gives us the network number for our next subnet, which is 183.17.2.0. We need eight host bits for Subnet B's 211 hosts (2 to the 8th power = 256 – 2 = 254), so we'll go with a mask of /24.

/24 mask	11111111	11111111	11111111	**00000000**
All-zeroes address: 183.17.2.0 /24	10110111	00010001	00000010	**00000000**
All-ones address: 183.17.2.255 /24	10110111	00010001	00000010	**11111111**

We know the drill – the address with all zeroes for the host bits is the subnet address, the address with all ones for the host bits is the broadcast address, and everything in the middle is a valid address for that subnet.

	Subnet Address	Valid Addresses	Broadcast Add.
Subnet A	183.17.0.0 /23	183.17.0.1 – 183.17.1.254 /23	183.17.1.255 /23
Subnet B	183.17.2.0 /24	183.17.2.1 – 183.17.2.254 /24	183.17.2.255 /24

The next address up from that broadcast address is 183.17.3.0, and we'll use that to begin Subnet C along with a subnet mask of 255.255.255.128 (/25), the tightest mask that allows for 78 host addresses. That mask leaves seven host bits, and 2 to the 7th power = 128 – 2 = 126.

/25 mask	11111111	11111111	11111111	**1**0000000
All-zeroes address: 183.17.3.0 /25	10110111	00010001	00000011	**0**0000000
All-ones address: 183.17.3.127 /25	10110111	00010001	00000011	**0**1111111

The all-zeroes address is 183.17.3.0 /25, the all-ones address is 183.17.3.127 /25, and everything in between is a valid address for Subnet C.

	Subnet Address	Valid Addresses	Broadcast Add.
Subnet A	183.17.0.0 /23	183.17.0.1 – 183.17.1.254 /23	183.17.1.255 /23
Subnet B	183.17.2.0 /24	183.17.2.1 – 183.17.2.254 /24	183.17.2.255 /24
Subnet C	183.17.3.0 /25	183.17.3.1 – 183.17.3.126 /25	183.17.3.127 /25

Next up is Subnet D, which begins with 183.17.3.128. This subnet needs at least 39 host addresses. We'll need six host bits to meet that requirement (2 to the 6th power = 64 – 2 = 62). The six-host-bit mask is 255.255.255.192 (/26).

/26 mask	11111111	11111111	11111111	**11**000000
All-zero address: 183.17.3.128	10110111	00010001	00000011	**10**000000
All-ones address: 183.17.3.191	10110111	00010001	00000011	**10**111111

The all-zeroes address is 183.17.3.128 /26, the all-ones address 183.17.3.191 /26, and everything in the middle is a valid address for Subnet D.

	Subnet Address	Valid Addresses	Broadcast Add.
Subnet A	183.17.0.0 /23	183.17.0.1 – 183.17.1.254 /23	183.17.1.255 /23
Subnet B	183.17.2.0 /24	183.17.2.1 – 183.17.2.254 /24	183.17.2.255 /24
Subnet C	183.17.3.0 /25	183.17.3.1 – 183.17.3.126 /25	183.17.3.127 /25
Subnet D	183.17.3.128 /26	183.17.3.129 – 183.17.3.190 /26	183.17.3.191 /26

Subnet E will begin with the next address up, 183.17.3.192. For our four hosts, we'll need three host bits (2 to the 3rd power = 8 – 2 = 6). We'll go with a mask of /29.

/29 mask	11111111	11111111	11111111	11111**000**
All-zero address: 183.17.3.192 /29	10110111	00010001	00000011	11000**000**
All-ones address: 183.17.3.199 /29	10110111	00010001	00000011	11000**111**

The all-zeroes address is 183.17.3.192 /29, the all-ones address is 183.17.3.199 /29, and the address range 183.17.3.193 – 183.17.3.198 /29 is the valid address range for Subnet E.

	Subnet Address	Valid Addresses	Broadcast Add.
Subnet A	183.17.0.0 /23	183.17.0.1 – 183.17.1.254 /23	183.17.1.255 /23
Subnet B	183.17.2.0 /24	183.17.2.1 – 183.17.2.254 /24	183.17.2.255 /24

Subnet C	183.17.3.0 /25	183.17.3.1 – 183.17.3.126 /25	183.17.3.127 /25
Subnet D	183.17.3.128 /26	183.17.3.129 – 183.17.3.190 /26	183.17.3.191 /26
Subnet E	183.17.3.192 /29	183.17.3.193 – 183.17.3.198 /29	183.17.3.199 /29

VLSM Exercise 2:

Given the 20.0.0.0 network, create six VLSM subnets that meet these requirements:

- Subnet A: 1047 hosts
- Subnet B: 834 hosts
- Subnet C: 422 hosts
- Subnet D: 99 hosts
- Subnet E: 7 hosts
- Subnet F: 5 hosts

With this Class A network, we have 8 network bits and 24 host bits. To give Subnet A room for at least 1047 host addresses, we'll need 11 host bits (2 to the 11th power = 2048 – 2 = 2046).   We'll borrow 13 of those 24 host bits for subnetting to leave those 11 host bits, resulting in the mask 255.255.248.0 (/21).

/21 mask	11111111	11111111	11111**000**	**00000000**
All-zeroes address: 20.0.0.0 /21	00010100	00000000	00000**000**	**00000000**
All-ones address: 20.0.7.255 /21	00010100	00000000	00000**111**	**11111111**

The all-zeroes address is the subnet address itself, 20.0.0.0 /21. The all-ones address gives us the broadcast address 20.0.7.255 /21. All addresses between those two are valid IP addresses.

	Subnet Address	Valid Addresses	Broadcast Address
Subnet A	20.0.0.0 /21	20.0.0.1 – 20.0.7.254 /21	20.0.7.255 /21

The very next address in sequence, 20.0.8.0, gives us the subnet number for Subnet B. We need room for a minimum of 834 host addresses on that subnet, so we'll need 10 host bits (2 to the 10th power = 1024 – 2 = 1022). We'll borrow 14 host bits for subnetting to leave those 10 host bits, giving us a subnet mask of 255.255.252.0 (/22).

/22 mask	11111111	11111111	111111**00**	**00000000**
All-zeroes address: 20.0.8.0 /22	00010100	00000000	000010**00**	**00000000**
All-ones address: 20.0.11.255 /22	00010100	00000000	000010**11**	**11111111**

The all-zeroes address is 20.0.8.0 /22, the all-ones address is 20.0.11.255 /22, and the range of valid addresses is 20.0.8.1 – 20.0.11.254 /22.

	Subnet Address	Valid Addresses	Broadcast Address
Subnet A	20.0.0.0 /21	20.0.0.1 – 20.0.7.254 /21	20.0.7.255 /21
Subnet B	20.0.8.0 /22	20.0.8.1 – 20.0.11.254 /22	20.0.11.255 /22

On to Subnet C, which begins with 20.0.12.0. We need 422 host addresses for that subnet, so we'll need to leave 9 host bits after subnetting (2 to the 9th power = 512 – 2 = 510 host addresses.) We'll need a 255.255.254.0 (/23) mask to leave those nine host bits.

/23 mask	11111111	11111111	1111111**0**	**00000000**
All-zeroes address: 20.0.12.0 /23	00010100	00000000	0000110**0**	**00000000**
All-ones address: 20.0.13.255 /23	00010100	00000000	0000110**1**	**11111111**

The all-zeroes address is 20.0.12.0 /23, the all-ones address is 20.0.13.255 /23, and the range of valid IP addresses for this subnet is 20.0.12.1 – 20.0.13.254 /23.

	Subnet Address	Valid Addresses	Broadcast Address
Subnet A	20.0.0.0 /21	20.0.0.1 – 20.0.7.254 /21	20.0.7.255 /21
Subnet B	20.0.8.0 /22	20.0.8.1 – 20.0.11.254 /22	20.0.11.255 /22
Subnet C	20.0.12.0 /23	20.0.12.1 – 20.0.13.254 /23	20.0.13.255 /23

Subnet D begins with 20.0.14.0, and we need a minimum of 99 host addresses for that subnet. Seven host bits will meet that requirement, as 2 to the 7th power = 128. Subtract the two, and you have 126 valid addresses on this subnet. To leave the seven host bits, we'll use a subnet mask of 255.255.255.128 (/25).

/25 mask	11111111	11111111	11111111	**1**0000000
All-zeroes address: 20.0.14.0 /25	00010100	00000000	00001110	**0**0000000
All-ones address: 20.0.14.127 /25	00010100	00000000	00001110	**0**1111111

The all-zeroes address is 20.0.14.0 /25, the all-ones address is 20.0.14.127 /25, and the range of valid addresses is 20.0.14.1 – 20.0.14.126 /25.

	Subnet Address	Valid Addresses	Broadcast Address
Subnet A	20.0.0.0 /21	20.0.0.1 – 20.0.7.254 /21	20.0.7.255 /21
Subnet B	20.0.8.0 /22	20.0.8.1 – 20.0.11.254 /22	20.0.11.255 /22
Subnet C	20.0.12.0 /23	20.0.12.1 – 20.0.13.254 /23	20.0.13.255 /23
Subnet D	20.0.14.0 /25	20.0.14.1 – 20.0.14.126 /25	20.0.14.127 /25

Two more subnets to go! We'll begin Subnet E with 20.0.14.128, and we need only seven host addresses there. We'll need to leave four host bits for seven addresses – three host bits won't quite do the job. 2 to the 4th power = 16 – 2 = 14 host addresses, while 2 to the 3rd power = 8 – 2 = 6 host addresses. To leave four host bits, we'll need a subnet mask of 255.255.255.240 (/28).

/28 mask	11111111	11111111	11111111	1111**0000**
All-zeroes address: 20.0.14.128 /28	00010100	00000000	00001110	1000**0000**
All-ones address: 20.0.14.143 /28	00010100	00000000	00001110	1000**1111**

The all-zeroes address is 20.0.14.128, the all-ones address is 20.0.14.143, and the valid address range is 20.0.14.129 – 142.

	Subnet Address	Valid Addresses	Broadcast Address
Subnet A	20.0.0.0 /21	20.0.0.1 – 20.0.7.254 /21	20.0.7.255 /21
Subnet B	20.0.8.0 /22	20.0.8.1 – 20.0.11.254 /22	20.0.11.255 /22
Subnet C	20.0.12.0 /23	20.0.12.1 – 20.0.13.254 /23	20.0.13.255 /23
Subnet D	20.0.14.0 /25	20.0.14.1 – 20.0.14.126 /25	20.0.14.127 /25
Subnet E	20.0.14.128 /28	20.0.14.129 – 20.0.14.142 /28	20.0.14.143 /28

Finally, Subnet F needs five host addresses. We can get away with three host bits here, since 2 to the 3rd power = 8 – 2 = 6 host addresses. A subnet mask of 255.255.255.248 (/29) leaves those precious three host bits. We'll start this subnet with 20.0.14.144, the next address up from the broadcast range of the last subnet.

/29 mask	11111111	11111111	11111111	11111**000**
All-zeroes address: 20.0.14.144 /29	00010100	00000000	00001110	10010**000**
All-ones address: 20.0.14.151 /29	00010100	00000000	00001110	10010**111**

The all-zeroes address is 20.0.14.144 /29, the all-ones address is 20.0.14.151 /29, and 20.0.14.145 – 150 /29 are your valid addresses for this subnet.

	Subnet Address	Valid Addresses	Broadcast Address
Subnet A	20.0.0.0 /21	20.0.0.1 – 20.0.7.254 /21	20.0.7.255 /21
Subnet B	20.0.8.0 /22	20.0.8.1 – 20.0.11.254 /22	20.0.11.255 /22
Subnet C	20.0.12.0 /23	20.0.12.1 – 20.0.13.254 /23	20.0.13.255 /23
Subnet D	20.0.14.0 /25	20.0.14.1 – 20.0.14.126 /25	20.0.14.127 /25
Subnet E	20.0.14.128 /28	20.0.14.129 – 20.0.14.142 /28	20.0.14.143 /28
Subnet F	20.0.14.144 /29	20.0.14.145 – 20.0.14.150 /29	20.0.14.151 /29

VLSM Exercise 3:

Working with the 170.13.0.0 network, create the following five subnets with the tightest possible mask while meeting these minimum requirements:

- Subnet A, 660 hosts
- Subnet B, 350 hosts
- Subnet C, 120 hosts
- Subnet D, 88 hosts
- Subnet E, 32 hosts

For Subnet A, we need enough host bits to allow for 660 host addresses, and that means 10 host bits (2 to the 10th power = 1024 – 2 = 1022 addresses). We're starting with a network mask of 255.255.0.0 with this Class B network, so to leave 10 host bits, we'll need to borrow six of the original sixteen host bits for subnetting. That gives us a subnet mask of 255.255.252.0 (/22).

/22 mask	11111111	11111111	111111**00**	**00000000**
All-zeroes address: 170.13.0.0 /22	10101010	00001101	000000**00**	**00000000**
All-ones address: 170.13.3.255 /22	10101010	00001101	000000**11**	**11111111**

The all-zeroes address is 170.13.0.0 /22, the all-ones address is 170.13.3.255 /22, and the range of valid addresses is 170.13.0.1 – 170.13.3.254 /22.

	Subnet Address	Valid Addresses	Broadcast Add.
Subnet A	170.13.0.0 /22	170.13.0.1 – 170.13.3.254 /22	170.13.3.255 /22

Subnet B begins with the next address up, 170.13.4.0, and we'll need to leave nine host bits to meet the requirement of 350 valid addresses on this subnet (2 to the 9th power = 512 - 2 = 510). That means a 23-bit subnet mask, expressed in dotted decimal as 255.255.254.0.

/23 mask	11111111	11111111	1111111**0**	**00000000**
All-zeroes address: 170.13.4.0 /23	10101010	00001101	0000010**0**	**00000000**
All-ones address: 170.13.5.255 /23	10101010	00001101	0000010**1**	**11111111**

The all-zeroes address is 170.13.4.0 /23, the all-ones address is 170.13.5.255 /23, and the range of valid addresses is 170.13.4.1 – 170.13.5.254 /23.

	Subnet Address	Valid Addresses	Broadcast Add.
Subnet A	170.13.0.0 /22	170.13.0.1 – 170.13.3.254 /22	170.13.3.255 /22
Subnet B	170.13.4.0 /23	170.13.4.1 – 170.13.5.254 /23	170.13.5.255 /23

Next up, Subnet C and its 120-host requirement. We'll need seven host bits to meet that requirement (2 to the 7th power = 128 – 2 = 126.) To leave seven host bits, we'll go with a subnet mask of /25 (255.255.255.128). This subnet will begin with 170.13.6.0, the next address up from the broadcast address of Subnet B.

/25 mask	11111111	11111111	11111111	10000000
All-zeroes address: 170.13.6.0 /25	10101010	00001101	00000110	00000000
All-ones address: 170.13.6.127 /25	10101010	00001101	00000110	01111111

The all-zeroes address is 170.13.6.0 /25, the all-ones address is 170.13.6.127 /25, and the range of valid addresses is 170.13.6.1 – 170.13.6.126 /25.

	Subnet Address	Valid Addresses	Broadcast Add.
Subnet A	170.13.0.0 /22	170.13.0.1 – 170.13.3.254 /22	170.13.3.255 /22
Subnet B	170.13.4.0 /23	170.13.4.1 – 170.13.5.254 /23	170.13.5.255 /23
Subnet C	170.13.6.0 /25	170.13.6.1 – 170.13.6.126 /25	170.13.6.127 /25

Subnet D needs at least 88 host addresses, which requires 7 host bits (2 to the 7th power = 128 – 2 = 126). We'll start that subnet with 170.13.6.128, the next address up from Subnet C's broadcast address. To leave the 7 host bits, we'll use a subnet mask of /25 (255.255.255.128).

/25 mask	11111111	11111111	11111111	10000000
All-zeroes address: 170.13.6.128 /25	10101010	00001101	00000110	10000000
All-ones address: 170.13.6.255 /25	10101010	00001101	00000110	11111111

The all-zeroes address is 170.13.6.128 /25, the all-ones address is 170.13.6.255 /25, and the range of valid addresses is 170.13.6.129 – 170.13.6.254 /25.

	Subnet Address	Valid Addresses	Broadcast Add.
Subnet A	170.13.0.0 /22	170.13.0.1 – 170.13.3.254 /22	170.13.3.255 /22
Subnet B	170.13.4.0 /23	170.13.4.1 – 170.13.5.254 /23	170.13.5.255
Subnet C	170.13.6.0 /25	170.13.6.1 – 170.13.6.126 /25	170.13.6.127 /25
Subnet D	170.13.6.128 /25	170.13.6.129 – 170.13.6.254 /25	170.13.6.255 /25

Finally, Subnet E needs 32 host addresses, and we'll need six host bits to make that happen (2 to the 6th power = 64 – 2 = 62). We'll go with a subnet mask of /26 to leave those six host bits. This subnet begins with 170.13.7.0, the next address up from Subnet D's broadcast address.

/26 mask	11111111	11111111	11111111	**11**000000
All-zeroes address: 170.13.7.0 /26	10101010	00001101	00000111	00**000000**
All-ones address: 170.13.7.63 /26	10101010	00001101	00000111	00**111111**

The all-zeroes address is 170.13.7.0 /26, the all-ones address is 170.13.7.63 /26, and the range of valid addresses on Subnet E is 170.13.7.1 – 170.13.7.62 /26.

	Subnet Address	Valid Addresses	Broadcast Add.
Subnet A	170.13.0.0 /22	170.13.0.1 – 170.13.3.254 /22	170.13.3.255 /22
Subnet B	170.13.4.0 /23	170.13.4.1 – 170.13.5.254 /23	170.13.5.255 /23
Subnet C	170.13.6.0 /25	170.13.6.1 – 170.13.6.126 /25	170.13.6.127 /25

| Subnet D | 170.13.6.128 /25 | 170.13.6.129 – 170.13.6.254 /25 | 170.13.6.255 /25 |
| Subnet E | 170.13.7.0 /26 | 170.13.7.1 – 170.13.7.62 /26 | 170.13.7.63 /26 |

VLSM Exercise 4:

Working with the 217.13.139.0 network, use VLSM to create the following subnets:

- Subnet A, 50 hosts
- Subnet B, 40 hosts
- Subnet C, 30 hosts
- Subnet D, 20 hosts
- Subnet E, 10 hosts

For Subnet A's 50-host requirement, we'll need 6 host bits, since 2 to the 6th power = 64 – 2 = 62 valid host addresses. With this Class C network, we're starting with 24 network bits and eight host bits, so we're just going to borrow two bits for subnetting, resulting in a /26 (255.255.255.192) subnet.

/26 mask	11111111	11111111	11111111	11**000000**
All-zeroes address: 217.13.139.0 /26	11011001	00001101	10001011	00**000000**
All-ones address: 217.13.139.63 /26	11011001	00001101	10001011	00**111111**

The all-zeroes address is 217.13.139.0 /26, and the all-ones address is 217.13.139.63 /26. Everything in between is fair game for host addressing.

	Subnet Address	Valid Addresses	Broadcast Address
Subnet A	217.13.139.0 /26	217.13.139.1 – 217.13.139.62 /26	217.13.139.63 /26

The next address up is 217.13.139.64, and that's the subnet number for Subnet B. That subnet requires 40 hosts, so we'll again need six host bits (2 to the 6th power = 64 – 2 = 62), which means we'll use the same mask.

/26 mask	11111111	11111111	11111111	11**000000**
All-zeroes address: 217.13.139.64 /26	11011001	00001101	10001011	01**000000**
All-ones address: 217.13.139.127 /26	11011001	00001101	10001011	01**111111**

The all-zeroes subnet number is 217.13.139.64 /26, and the all-ones broadcast address is 217.13.139.127 /26. Everything in the middle is a valid address for Subnet B.

	Subnet Address	Valid Addresses	Broadcast Address
Subnet A	217.13.139.0 /26	217.13.139.1 – 217.13.139.62 /26	217.13.139.63 /26
Subnet B	217.13.139.64 /26	217.13.139.65 – 217.13.139.126 /26	217.13.139.127 /26

We move up one address to 217.13.139.128, which is the subnet number for Subnet C. We need a minimum of 30 hosts here, and the lowest number of host bits that gives us that many hosts is five (2 to the 5th power = 32 – 2 = 30, just what we need.) A subnet mask of /27 will do nicely here.

/27 mask	11111111	11111111	11111111	111**00000**
All-zeroes address: 217.13.139.128 /27	11011001	00001101	10001011	100**00000**

All-ones address: 217.13.139.159 /27	11011001	00001101	10001011	100**11111**

The subnet number is 217.13.139.128 /27, the all-ones broadcast address for that subnet is 217.13.139.159 /27, and the range of acceptable host IP addresses for Subnet C is everything in between.

	Subnet Address	Valid Addresses	Broadcast Address
Subnet A	217.13.139.0 /26	217.13.139.1 – 217.13.139.62 /26	217.13.139.63 /26
Subnet B	217.13.139.64 /26	217.13.139.65 – 217.13.139.126 /26	217.13.139.127 /26
Subnet C	217.13.139.128 /27	217.13.139.129 – 217.13.139.158 /27	217.13.139.159 /27

Subnet D will start with 217.13.139.160, and we need 20 host addresses for that subnet. We'll need five host bits again (2 to the 5th power = 32 – 2 = 30), so we'll use the same mask as we used for Subnet C.

/27 mask	11111111	11111111	11111111	111**00000**
All-zeroes address: 217.13.139.160 /27	11011001	00001101	10001011	101**00000**
All-ones address: 217.13.139.191 /27	11011001	00001101	10001011	101**11111**

The subnet address is 217.13.139.160 /27, the all-ones broadcast address is 217.13.139.191/27, and the valid address range is 217.13.139.161 – 190 /27.

	Subnet Address	Valid Addresses	Broadcast Address
Subnet A	217.13.139.0 /26	217.13.139.1 – 217.13.139.62 /26	217.13.139.63 /26
Subnet B	217.13.139.64 /26	217.13.139.65 – 217.13.139.126 /26	217.13.139.127 /26
Subnet C	217.13.139.128 /27	217.13.139.129 – 217.13.139.158 /27	217.13.139.159 /27
Subnet D	217.13.139.160 /27	217.13.139.161 – 217.13.139.190 /27	217.13.139.191 /27

Finally, Subnet E will start with 217.13.139.192, and we need 10 valid host addresses for that subnet. Four host bits will make that happen, as 2 to the 4th power = 16, and after subtracting the two invalid addresses, we have 14 valid addresses left on this subnet. A /28 mask will do the job.

/28 mask	11111111	11111111	11111111	1111**0000**
All-zeroes address: 217.13.139.192 /28	11011001	00001101	10001011	1100**0000**
All-ones address: 217.13.139.207 /28	11011001	00001101	10001011	1100**1111**

The subnet number is 217.13.139.192 /28, the broadcast address for this subnet is 217.13.139.207 /28, and the valid address range is 217.13.139.193 – 217.13.139.206 /28.

	Subnet Address	Valid Addresses	Broadcast Address
Subnet A	217.13.139.0 /26	217.13.139.1 – 217.13.139.62 /26	217.13.139.63 /26
Subnet B	217.13.139.64 /26	217.13.139.65 – 217.13.139.126 /26	217.13.139.127 /26
Subnet C	217.13.139.128 /27	217.13.139.129 – 217.13.139.158 /27	217.13.139.159 /27
Subnet D	217.13.139.160 /27	217.13.139.161 – 217.13.139.190 /27	217.13.139.191 /27
Subnet E	217.13.139.192 /28	217.13.139.193 – 217.13.139.206 /28	217.13.139.207 /28

Watch those masks on your exam, especially with VLSM questions. "217.13.139.192" is not the same as "217.13.139.192 /28". Gotta have the mask!

VLSM Exercise 5:

Working with the Class B 160.20.0.0 network, let's create that meet these varying host-per-subnet requirements:

- Subnet A, 745 hosts
- Subnet B, 512 hosts
- Subnet C, 279 hosts
- Subnet D, 193 hosts
- Subnet E, 84 hosts

We'll need 10 host bits for Subnet A since that's the minimum number of host bits that give us at least 745 hosts (2 to the 10th power = 1024 – 2 = 1022). The mask we need here is /22.

/22 mask	11111111	11111111	111111**00**	**00000000**
All-zeroes address: 160.20.0.0 /22	10100000	00010100	000000**00**	**00000000**
All-ones address: 160.20.3.255 /22	10100000	00010100	000000**11**	**11111111**

Subnet A's subnet address is 160.20.0.0 /22, the all-ones address is 160.20.3.255 /22, and everything between the two is a valid host address.

	Subnet Address	Host Addresses	Broadcast Address
Subnet A	160.20.0.0 /22	160.20.0.1 – 160.20.3.254 /22	160.20.3.255 /22

Next up is Subnet B. That subnet needs at least 512 host addresses, so we again need to have 10 host bits after subnetting. While 2 to the 9th power does equal 512, we have to subtract the subnet and broadcast addresses from that range, so nine host bits would leave us with only 510 host addresses. We begin with 160.20.4.0, just one address up from Subnet A's broadcast address.

/22 mask	11111111	11111111	111111**00**	**00000000**
All-zeroes address: 160.20.4.0 /22	10100000	00010100	000001**00**	**00000000**
All-ones address: 160.20.7.255 /22	10100000	00010100	000001**11**	**11111111**

The subnet number is 160.20.4.0 /22, the broadcast address is 160.20.7.255 /22, and the range of valid addresses is everything in between.

	Subnet Address	Host Addresses	Broadcast Address
Subnet A	160.20.0.0 /22	160.20.0.1 – 160.20.3.254 /22	160.20.3.255 /22
Subnet B	160.20.4.0 /22	160.20.4.1 – 160.20.7.254 /22	160.20.7.255 /22

Subnet C begins with 160.20.8.0, and we'll need nine host bits to meet the requirement of 279 hosts (2 to the 9th power = 512 – 2 = 510.) The /23 mask gets the job done here.

/23 mask	11111111	11111111	11111110	00000000
All-zeroes address: 160.20.8.0 /23	10100000	00010100	0000100**0**	**00000000**
All-ones address: 160.20.9.255 /23	10100000	00010100	0000100**1**	**11111111**

The subnet number is 160.20.8.0 /23, the broadcast address is 160.20.9.255 /23, and you know the deal with the range of valid addresses.

	Subnet Address	Host Addresses	Broadcast Address
Subnet A	160.20.0.0 /22	160.20.0.1 – 160.20.3.254 /22	160.20.3.255 /22
Subnet B	160.20.4.0 /22	160.20.4.1 – 160.20.7.254 /22	160.20.7.255 /22
Subnet C	160.20.8.0 /23	160.20.8.1 – 160.20.9.254 /23	160.20.9.255 /23

Subnet D begins with 160.20.10.0 and will need 8 host bits due to its requirement of 193 hosts (2 to the 8th power = 256 − 2 = 254 host addresses). A subnet mask of /24 will do nicely.

/24 mask	11111111	11111111	11111111	00000000
All-zeroes address: 160.20.10.0 /24	10100000	00010100	00001010	**00000000**
All-ones address: 160.20.10.255 /24	10100000	00010100	00001010	**11111111**

Our subnet number is 160.20.10.0 /24, the broadcast address is 160.20.10.255 /24, and the range of valid addresses is everything in between.

	Subnet Address	Host Addresses	Broadcast Address
Subnet A	160.20.0.0 /22	160.20.0.1 − 160.20.3.254 /22	160.20.3.255 /22
Subnet B	160.20.4.0 /22	160.20.4.1 − 160.20.7.254 /22	160.20.7.255 /22
Subnet C	160.20.8.0 /23	160.20.8.1 − 160.20.9.254 /23	160.20.9.255 /23
Subnet D	160.20.10.0 /24	160.20.10.1 − 160.20.10.254 /24	160.20.10.255 /24

Finally, Subnet E will begin with 160.20.11.0, and it requires 84 valid addresses. Seven host bits yield 126 host addresses (2 to the 7th power = 128 − 2 = 126), so we'll go with a mask of /25.

/25 mask	11111111	11111111	11111111	1**0000000**
All-zeroes address: 160.20.11.0 /25	10100000	00010100	00001011	0**0000000**
All-ones address: 160.20.11.127 /25	10100000	00010100	00001011	0**1111111**

Our final subnet number is 160.20.11.0 /25, the broadcast address is 160.20.11.127 /25, and the range of valid addresses is the same as it ever was.

	Subnet Address	Host Addresses	Broadcast Address
Subnet A	160.20.0.0 /22	160.20.0.1 – 160.20.3.254 /22	160.20.3.255 /22
Subnet B	160.20.4.0 /22	160.20.4.1 – 160.20.7.254 /22	160.20.7.255 /22
Subnet C	160.20.8.0 /23	160.20.8.1 – 160.20.9.254 /23	160.20.9.255 /23
Subnet D	160.20.10.0 /24	160.20.10.1 – 160.20.10.254 /24	160.20.10.255 /24
Subnet E	160.20.11.0 /25	160.20.11.1 – 160.20.11.126 /25	160.20.11.127 /25

Great work!   Let your brain cool off a bit and then we'll have a go with route summarization.

CHAPTER 20:

Manual Route Summarization

You won't perform manual route summarization at the same time you subnet your network, but the skills involved in summarization and subnetting are *very* similar. In fact, they're so similar that it's an excellent idea to learn and practice route summarization at the same time you're sharpening your subnetting skills. You'll run into summarization situations throughout your networking career – not to mention your certification exams.

Manual route summarization is a powerful skill that brings these benefits to our network:

- The routing tables are smaller, making the entire routing process faster.

- Since the tables are smaller, the load on the CPU from the routing process is lessened.

- Routing updates themselves are smaller.

- The more-specific network numbers are hidden, a small boost to our overall network security plan.

- The impact of flapping links on the rest of the network is lessened.

In this lab, R1 is advertising seven routes to its EIGRP neighbor, R2. *You do not need experience with EIGRP to master manual route summarization;* I'm using this lab to illustrate the power of this feature and give you a scenario where you might find it helpful.

R2 sees all seven routes.

```
R2#show ip route eigrp
     100.0.0.0/16 is subnetted, 7 subnets
D       100.1.0.0 [90/2297856] via 172.12.123.1, 00:00:31, Serial0/1/0
D       100.2.0.0 [90/2297856] via 172.12.123.1, 00:00:31, Serial0/1/0
D       100.3.0.0 [90/2297856] via 172.12.123.1, 00:00:31, Serial0/1/0
D       100.4.0.0 [90/2297856] via 172.12.123.1, 00:00:31, Serial0/1/0
D       100.5.0.0 [90/2297856] via 172.12.123.1, 00:00:31, Serial0/1/0
D       100.6.0.0 [90/2297856] via 172.12.123.1, 00:00:31, Serial0/1/0
D       100.7.0.0 [90/2297856] via 172.12.123.1, 00:00:31, Serial0/1/0
```

There's nothing technically wrong with that table, but we'd like to keep our routing tables as complete and concise as possible. Manual route summarization can knock those seven routes down to *one line.* We begin by breaking each route down into binary strings. The next step is to work from left to right and identify the common bits of all the routes.

	1st Octet	2nd Octet	3rd Octet	4th Octet
100.1.0.0	**01100100**	**00000**001	(all zeroes)	(all zeroes)
100.2.0.0	**01100100**	**00000**010		
100.3.0.0	**01100100**	**00000**011		
100.4.0.0	**01100100**	**00000**100		
100.5.0.0	**01100100**	**00000**101		
100.6.0.0	**01100100**	**00000**110		
100.7.0.0	**01100100**	**00000**111		

The decimal value of the common bits yields the summary route, and the number of common bits yields the summary mask. We can see that all seven routes have the first 13 bits in common; at that point, they become "non-common" as the first three routes have a zero for the 14th bit and the last four routes have a 1 for that same bit. The value of the common bits is 100.0.0.0.

1st Octet	2nd Octet	3rd Octet	4th Octet	Summary
01100100	**00000xxx**	xxxxxxxx	xxxxxxxx	100.0.0.0

Every summary route needs a mask; otherwise, it's not a summary route. The number of common bits gives us that mask, expressed /13 in prefix notation and 255.248.0.0 in dotted decimal. Apply it to the advertising interface, and you're all set.

```
R1(config)#int serial 0/1/0
R1(config-if)#ip summary-address ?
  eigrp   Enhanced Interior Gateway Routing Protocol (EIGRP)
  rip     Routing Information Protocol (RIP)

R1(config-if)#ip summary-address eigrp ?
  <1-65535>  AS number

R1(config-if)#ip summary-address eigrp 100 ?
  A.B.C.D  IP address

R1(config-if)#ip summary-address eigrp 100 100.0.0.0 ?
  A.B.C.D  IP network mask

R1(config-if)#ip summary-address eigrp 100 100.0.0.0 255.248.0.0

%DUAL-5-NBRCHANGE: EIGRP-IPv4 100: Neighbor 172.12.123.3 (Serial0/1/0) is
resync: summary configured
  %DUAL-5-NBRCHANGE: EIGRP-IPv4 100: Neighbor 172.12.123.2 (Serial0/1/0) is
resync: summary configured
```

The routing table on R2 reflects the summary route only. R1 is no longer advertising the more-specific routes on Serial 0/1/0. Having one line that matches all eight of the previously visible subnets makes R2's routing process more efficient. Keep those tables complete and concise!

```
R2#show ip route eigrp
       100.0.0.0/13 is subnetted, 1 subnets
D         100.0.0.0 [90/2297856] via 172.12.123.1, 00:00:43, Serial0/1/0
```

A quick note here for those who have studied EIGRP: There's a new EIGRP route in an unexpected place – R1.

```
R1#show ip route eigrp
D         100.0.0.0/13 is a summary, 00:02:42, Null0
```

On the summarizing router, the summary route is seen as a route to "Null0". Basically, this is a route to the trash can. If a packet comes in that doesn't match one of the seven more-specific routes that have been summarized, that packet will be dropped. This EIGRP default behavior helps to prevent routing loops.

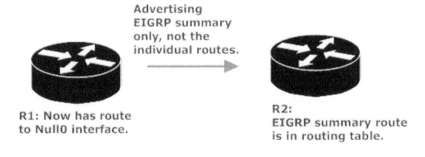

R1: Now has route to Null0 interface.

Advertising EIGRP summary only, not the individual routes.

R2: EIGRP summary route is in routing table.

Let's get some more work in on route summarization with this set of routes. Each route has a /16 mask.

- 10.16.0.0
- 10.17.0.0
- 10.18.0.0
- 10.19.0.0

- 10.20.0.0
- 10.21.0.0
- 10.22.0.0
- 10.23.0.0

	1st Octet	2nd Octet	3rd Octet	4th Octet
10.16.0.0	**00001010**	**00010**000	(all zeroes)	(all zeroes)
10.17.0.0	**00001010**	**00010**001		
10.18.0.0	**00001010**	**00010**010		
10.19.0.0	**00001010**	**00010**011		
10.20.0.0	**00001010**	**00010**100		
10.21.0.0	**00001010**	**00010**101		
10.22.0.0	**00001010**	**00010**110		
10.23.0.0	**00001010**	**00010**111		

Convert the common bits back to decimal, and we have 10.16.0.0. The all-important mask is /13 (255.248.0.0), so the full summary is 10.16.0.0 /13 or 10.16.0.0 255.248.0.0. *Watch the mask on exam day!*

Let's hit another set of routes, each with a /24 mask.
- 172.13.8.0
- 172.13.9.0
- 172.13.10.0
- 172.13.11.0
- 172.13.12.0
- 172.13.13.0
- 172.13.14.0
- 172.13.15.0

	1st Octet	2nd Octet	3rd Octet	4th Octet
172.13.8.0	**10101100**	**00001101**	**00001**000	(all zeroes)
172.13.9.0	**10101100**	**00001101**	**00001**001	
172.13.10.0	**10101100**	**00001101**	**00001**010	
172.13.11.0	**10101100**	**00001101**	**00001**011	
172.13.12.0	**10101100**	**00001101**	**00001**100	
172.13.13.0	**10101100**	**00001101**	**00001**101	
172.13.14.0	**10101100**	**00001101**	**00001**110	
172.13.15.0	**10101100**	**00001101**	**00001**111	

The routes have 21 common bits, shown in bold. Convert the common bits back to decimal, and you have your summary route, 172.13.8.0 255.255.248.0 (/21).

There's one small danger with summarizing routes you should be aware of, and that'll become apparent when we summarize the following routes, each with a /24 mask.

- 182.14.16.0
- 182.14.17.0
- 182.14.18.0
- 182.14.19.0
- 182.14.20.0
- 182.14.21.0

	1st Octet	2nd Octet	3rd Octet	4th Octet
182.14.16.0	**10110110**	**00001110**	**00010**000	(all zeroes)
182.14.17.0	**10110110**	**00001110**	**00010**001	
182.14.18.0	**10110110**	**00001110**	**00010**010	
182.14.19.0	**10110110**	**00001110**	**00010**011	
182.14.20.0	**10110110**	**00001110**	**00010**100	
182.14.21.0	**10110110**	**00001110**	**00010**101	

The common bits are 10110110 00001110 00010xxx xxxxxxxx, so our summary route is 182.14.16.0 /21, right? Right!

The problem is that two routes *not* posed in the question, 182.14.22.0 and 182.14.23.0, have those same first 21 bits.

	1st Octet	2nd Octet	3rd Octet	4th Octet
182.14.16.0	**10110110**	**00001110**	**00010**000	(all 0s in each)
182.14.17.0	**10110110**	**00001110**	**00010**001	
182.14.18.0	**10110110**	**00001110**	**00010**010	
182.14.19.0	**10110110**	**00001110**	**00010**011	
182.14.20.0	**10110110**	**00001110**	**00010**100	
182.14.21.0	**10110110**	**00001110**	**00010**101	
182.14.22.0	**10110110**	**00001110**	**00010**110	
182.14.23.0	**10110110**	**00001110**	**00010**111	

If those two particular routes aren't in use in your network, you'd be okay with that summary...

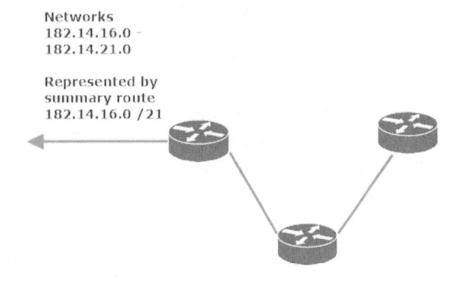

Networks
182.14.16.0 –
182.14.21.0

Represented by
summary route
182.14.16.0 /21

... but things change, and someone could use one or both of those two routes in another part of your network, which could screw around with your routing.

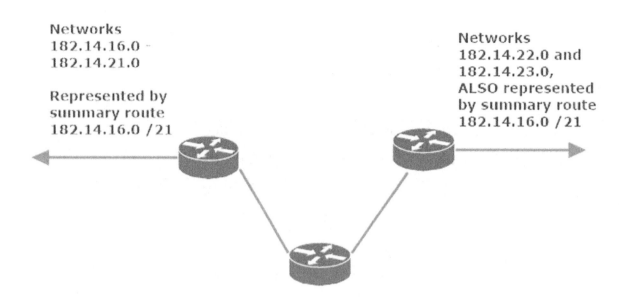

Networks
182.14.16.0 -
182.14.21.0

Represented by
summary route
182.14.16.0 /21

Networks
182.14.22.0 and
182.14.23.0,
ALSO represented
by summary route
182.14.16.0 /21

A great way to spot this potential issue is to examine the **non**-common bits of the octet where the mask ends. If those bits aren't all ones for the last route summarized, you should reconsider the summary route. For example, in this exercise, the non-common bits of the third octet stopped at "101". That's a dead giveaway that this summarization includes routes that you didn't include in the ones you wrote out.

	1st Octet	2nd Octet	3rd Octet	4th Octet
182.14.16.0	**10110110**	**00001110**	**00010**000	(all 0s in each)
182.14.17.0	**10110110**	**00001110**	**00010**001	
182.14.18.0	**10110110**	**00001110**	**00010**010	
182.14.19.0	**10110110**	**00001110**	**00010**011	
182.14.20.0	**10110110**	**00001110**	**00010**100	
182.14.21.0	**10110110**	**00001110**	**00010**101	

If you gave me those six routes in a real-world networking situation, I would summarize the first four routes and continue to advertise 182.14.20.0 and 182.14.21.0 separately. That still shrinks our routing table by 50%, from six routes to three, and we don't have the chance of suboptimal routing.

	1st Octet	2nd Octet	3rd Octet	4th Octet
182.14.16.0	**10110110**	**00001110**	**000100**00	(all 0s in each)
182.14.17.0	**10110110**	**00001110**	**000100**01	
182.14.18.0	**10110110**	**00001110**	**000100**10	
182.14.19.0	**10110110**	**00001110**	**000100**11	

The summary here is 182.14.16.0 255.255.252.0 (/22).

Head over to my CCNA Tutorials page for immediate access to tons of free info (including this EIGRP course), all designed to help you pass the exam and develop your real-world networking skills!

http://bit.ly/FreeCCNATutorials

Speaking of free, you can never get enough subnetting practice, so I've included three bonus sections of assorted subnetting questions in the next three sections – all with illustrated answers, of course. Dig in, and thank you for making my work part of your success story!

Chris Bryant

CCIE #12933

"The Computer Certification Bulldog"

Website: https://www.thebryantadvantage.com

Twitter: https://www.twitter.com/ccie12933

Facebook: https://www.facebook.com/ccie12933/

LinkedIn: https://www.linkedin.com/in/bulldogchrisbryant/

YouTube: https://www.youtube.com/user/ccie12933

CCNA Video Boot Camp: http://bit.ly/CCNA2019

Subnetting Success Exam Pack: http://bit.ly/SubnetSuccess

CHAPTER 21:

Bonus Review Exercise Set #1

Warm-Up:

Convert the binary string 00101100 to decimal.

Convert the binary string 11011001 to decimal.

Convert the decimal 79 to binary.

Convert the decimal 183 to binary.

Converting 00101100 to decimal:

128	64	32	16	8	4	2	1	Total
0	0	1	0	1	1	0	0	44

Converting 11011001 to decimal:

128	64	32	16	8	4	2	1	Total
1	1	0	1	1	0	0	1	217

Converting 79 to a binary string:

	128	64	32	16	8	4	2	1
79	0	1	0	0	1	1	1	1

Converting 183 to a binary string:

	128	64	32	16	8	4	2	1
183	1	0	1	1	0	1	1	1

How many valid subnets exist on each of the following networks?
- 172.13.0.0 /22
- 80.0.0.0 /16
- 193.17.126.0 /27
- 17.0.0.0 255.255.224.0
- 200.1.1.0 255.255.255.240
- 150.1.0.0 255.255.252.0

172.13.0.0 /22:
Subtract the network mask length from the subnet mask length and you're (almost) gold. This Class B network has a network mask of /16. 22 − 16 = 6 subnet bits. 2 to the 6th power = 64 valid subnets.

80.0.0.0 /16:
Class A network with a network mask of /8. 16 − 8 = 8 subnet bits. 2 to the 8th power = 256 valid subnets.

193.17.126.0 /27:
Class C network with a network mask of /24. 27 − 24 = 3 subnet bits. 2 to the 3rd power = 8 valid subnets.

17.0.0.0 255.255.224.0:
Class A network, network mask of /8. This dotted decimal mask has its first 19 bits set to one (/19). 19 − 8 = 11 subnet bits. 2 to the 11th power = 2048 valid subnets.

200.1.1.0 255.255.255.240:
Class C network, network mask of /24. This dotted decimal mask has its first 28 bits set to one (/28). 28 − 24 = 4 subnet bits. 2 to the 4th power = 16 valid subnets.

150.1.0.0 255.255.252.0:
Class B network, network mask of /16. This dotted decimal mask has its first 22 bits set to one (/22). 22 − 16 = 6 subnet bits. 2 to the 6^{h} power = 64 valid subnets.

How many valid host addresses exist on the following subnets?
- 70.0.0.0 /21
- 140.1.0.0 /25

- 220.4.3.0 /28
- 40.0.0.0 255.255.248.0
- 160.6.0.0 255.255.254.0
- 200.1.4.0 255.255.255.252

70.0.0.0 /21:
We need the number of host bits, and we get that by subtracting the given subnet mask length from 32. Here, 32 – 21 = 11 host bits. 2 to the 11th power = 2048. 2048 – 2 invalid addresses (first and last in range) = 2046 valid addresses per subnet.

140.1.0.0 /25:
32 – 25 = 7 host bits. 2 to the 7th power = 128. 128 – 2 invalid addresses = 126 valid addresses per subnet.

220.4.3.0 /28
32 – 28 = 4 host bits. 2 to the 4th power = 16. 16 – 2 = 14 valid addresses per subnet.

40.0.0.0 255.255.248.0:
In prefix notation, this mask is /21. 32 – 21 = 11 host bits. 2 to the 11th power = 2048. Take off those two invalid addresses and you have 2046 valid addresses per subnet.

160.6.0.0 255.255.254.0:
In prefix notation, this mask is /23. 32 – 23 = 9. 2 to the 9th power = 512. Take off the two and you have 510 valid addresses per subnet.

200.1.4.0 255.255.255.252
In prefix notation, this mask is /30. 32 – 30 = 2. 2 to the 2nd power = 4. Remove the two invalid addresses and you have 2 valid addresses per subnet.

Determine the broadcast address and the range of valid IP addresses for each of the following subnets.
- 91.0.0.0 /17
- 142.10.0.0 /23
- 199.3.17.0 255.255.255.128
- 10.0.0.0 255.252.0.0

91.0.0.0 /17:

	Octet 1	Octet 2	Octet 3	Octet 4
91.0.0.0 /17: Subnet Address, All host bits set to zero.	01011011	00000000	0**0000000**	**00000000**
B'Cast Address, all host bits set to one.	01011011	00000000	0**1111111**	**11111111**

Subnet address: 91.0.0.0 /17

Range of valid addresses: 91.0.0.1 – 91.0.127.254 /17

Broadcast address: 91.0.127.255 /17

142.10.0.0 /23:

	Octet 1	Octet 2	Octet 3	Octet 4
142.10.0.0 /23 Subnet Address, All host bits set to zero.	10001110	00001010	0000000**0**	**00000000**
B'Cast Address, all host bits set to one.	10001110	00001010	0000000**1**	**11111111**

Subnet address: 142.10.0.0 /23

Range of valid addresses: 142.10.0.1 – 142.10.1.254 /23

Broadcast address: 142.10.1.255 /23

199.3.17.0 255.255.255.128:

	Octet 1	Octet 2	Octet 3	Octet 4
199.3.17.0 255.255.255.128: Subnet Address, All host bits set to zero.	11000111	00000011	00010001	0**0000000**
B'Cast Address, all host bits set to one.	11000111	00000011	00010001	0**1111111**

Subnet address: 199.3.17.0 255.255.255.128 (/25)

Range of valid addresses: 199.3.17.1 – 199.3.17.126 255.255.255.128

Broadcast address: 199.3.17.127 255.255.255.128

10.0.0.0 255.252.0.0

	Octet 1		Octet 2	Octet 3	Octet 4
10.0.0.0 255.252.0.0: Subnet Address, All host bits set to zero.	00001010		000000**00**	**00000000**	**00000000**
B'Cast Address, all host bits set to one.	00001010		000000**11**	**11111111**	**11111111**

Subnet address: 10.0.0.0 255.252.0.0 (/14)

Range of valid addresses: 10.0.0.1 – 10.3.255.254 255.252.0.0

Broadcast address: 10.3.255.255 255.252.0.0

https://bit.ly/FreeCCNATutorials

CHAPTER 22:

Bonus Review Exercise Set #2:

How many valid subnets exist on each of the following networks?

- 50.0.0.0 /18
- 30.0.0.0 /20
- 145.1.0.0 /23
- 200.4.5.0 /28
- 205.3.1.0 /29

50.0.0.0 /18:
Class A network with a /8 network mask. 18 – 8 = 10 subnet bits. 2 to the 10th power = 1024 valid subnets.

30.0.0.0 /20
Class A network with a /8 network mask. 20 – 8 = 12 subnet bits. 2 to the 12th power = 4096 valid subnets.

145.1.0.0 /23
Class B network with a /16 network mask. 23 – 16 = 7 subnet bits. 2 to the 7th power = 128 valid subnets.

200.4.5.0 /28
Class C network with a /24 network mask. 28 – 24 = 4 subnet bits. 2 to the 4th power = 16 valid subnets.

205.3.1.0 /29
Class C network with a /24 network mask. 29 – 24 = 5 subnet bits. 2 to the 5th power = 32 valid subnets.

How many valid host addresses exist on each of the following subnets?

- 37.0.0.0 /21
- 170.3.0.0 /24
- 189.17.0.0 /26
- 199.3.9.0 /25
- 45.0.0.0 /20
- 214.13.19.0 /27

37.0.0.0 /21
32 – 21 = 11 host bits. 2 to the 11th power – 2 = 2046 valid addresses.

170.3.0.0 /24
32 – 24 = 8 host bits. 2 to the 8th power – 2 = 254 valid addresses.

189.17.0.0 /26
32 – 26 = 6 host bits. 2 to the 6th power – 2 = 62 valid addresses.

199.3.9.0 /25
32 – 25 = 7 host bits.   2 to the 7th power – 2 = 126 valid addresses.

45.0.0.0 /20
32 – 20 – 12 host bits. 2 to the 12th power – 2 = 4094 valid addresses.

214.13.19.0 /27
32 – 27 = 5 host bits. 2 to the 5th power – 2 = 30 valid addresses.

Determine the broadcast address and the range of available (and valid!) IP addresses for each of the following subnets.

- 35.0.0.0 /23
- 152.42.0.0 /27
- 205.2.47.0 /26
- 78.0.0.0 /10
- 211.17.92.192 /28
- 138.14.0.0 /19

35.0.0.0 /23:

	Octet 1	Octet 2	Octet 3	Octet 4
35.0.0.0 /23: Subnet Address, All host bits set to zero.	00100011	00000000	0000000**0**	**00000000**
B'Cast Address, all host bits set to one.	00100011	00000000	0000000**1**	**11111111**

Subnet address: 35.0.0.0 /23

Range of valid addresses: 35.0.0.1 – 35.0.1.254 /23

Broadcast address: 35.0.1.255 /23

152.42.0.0 /27:

	Octet 1	Octet 2	Octet 3	Octet 4
152.42.0.0 /27 Subnet Address, All host bits set to zero.	10011000	00101010	00000000	000**00000**
B'Cast Address, all host bits set to one.	10011000	00101010	00000000	000**11111**

Subnet address: 152.42.0.0 /27

Range of valid addresses: 152.42.0.1 – 152.42.0.30 /27

Broadcast address: 152.42.0.31 /27

205.2.47.0 /26:

	Octet 1	Octet 2	Octet 3	Octet 4
205.2.47.0 /26: Subnet Address, All host bits set to zero.	11001101	00000010	00101111	00**000000**
B'Cast Address, all host bits set to one.	11001101	00000010	00101111	00**111111**

Subnet address: 205.2.47.0 /26

Range of valid addresses: 205.2.47.1 – 205.2.47.62 /26

Broadcast address: 205.2.47.63 /26

78.0.0.0 /10:

	Octet 1	Octet 2	Octet 3	Octet 4
78.0.0.0 /10: Subnet Address, All host bits set to zero.	01001110	00**000000**	**00000000**	**00000000**
B'Cast Address, all host bits set to one.	01001110	00**111111**	**11111111**	**11111111**

Subnet address: 78.0.0.0 /10

Range of valid addresses: 78.0.0.1 – 78.63.255.254 /10

Broadcast address: 78.63.255.255 /10

211.17.92.192 /28:

	Octet 1	Octet 2	Octet 3	Octet 4
211.17.92.192 /28: Subnet Address, All host bits set to zero.	11010011	00010001	01011100	1100**0000**
B'Cast Address, all host bits set to one.	11010011	00010001	01011100	1100**1111**

Subnet address: 211.17.92.192 /28

Range of valid addresses: 211.17.92.193 – 211.17.92.206 /28

Broadcast address: 211.17.92.207 /28

138.14.0.0 /19:

	Octet 1	Octet 2	Octet 3	Octet 4
Subnet Address, All host bits set to zero.	10001010	00001110	000**00000**	**00000000**
B'Cast Address, all host bits set to one.	10001010	00001110	000**11111**	**11111111**

Subnet address: 138.14.0.0 /19

Range of valid addresses: 138.14.0.1 – 138.14.31.254 /19

Broadcast address: 138.14.31.255 /19

Time for subnetting!

You're subnetting the 135.28.0.0 network. You need at least 490 subnets and at least 600 hosts per subnet. What mask or masks, if any, will accomplish this?

This Class B network gives us 16 host bits to work with.

	1st Octet	2nd Octet	3rd Octet	4th Octet
Network Bits	11111111	11111111		
Subnet Bits				
Host Bits			00000000	00000000

We need to borrow at least nine host bits for subnetting to give us at least 490 subnets (2 to the 9th power = 512).

	1st Octet	2nd Octet	3rd Octet	4th Octet
Network Bits	11111111	11111111		
Subnet Bits			11111111	1
Host Bits				0000000

That leaves seven host bits, which gives us 126 valid addresses per subnet (2 to the 7th power -2). That violates the second requirement. That's as many valid addresses per subnet as you can have while still having at least 490 valid subnets, so there is no mask that will meet both requirements.

You're subnetting the 192.13.17.0 network, and you want to have at least seven subnets while maximizing the number of valid host addresses per subnet. What's the best mask for the job?

Class C networks come with 24 network bits and eight host bits. To meet these two requirements, we need to borrow as few host bits as possible while still ending up with at least seven subnets.

	1st Octet	2nd Octet	3rd Octet	4th Octet
Network Bits	11111111	11111111	11111111	
Subnet Bits				
Host Bits				00000000

The lowest number of subnet bits that give us seven subnets is three (2 to the 3rd power = 8). The resulting mask is 255.255.255.224 (/27).

	1st Octet	2nd Octet	3rd Octet	4th Octet
Network Bits	11111111	11111111	11111111	
Subnet Bits				111
Host Bits				00000

CHAPTER 23:

Bonus Review Exercise Set #3

How many valid subnets are there on each of the following subnets?
- 19.0.0.0 /19
- 144.1.0.0 /25
- 210.3.10.0 255.255.255.240

19.0.0.0 /19
Class A network, /8 network mask. 19 – 8 = 11 subnet bits. 2 to the 11th power = 2048 valid subnets.

144.1.0.0 /25 network
Class B network, /16 network mask. 25 – 16 = 9 subnet bits. 2 to the 9th power = 512 valid subnets.

210.3.10.0 255.255.255.240
Class C network, /24 network mask. The 255.255.255.240 mask is equivalent to a /28 in prefix notation. 28 – 24 = 4 subnet bits. 2 to the 4th power = 16 valid subnets.

How many valid host addresses are there in each of these subnets?
- 181.14.0.0 /21
- 199.17.30.0 255.255.255.248
- 47.0.0.0 /255.255.255.128

181.14.0.0 /21
32 – 21 = 11 host bits. 2 to the 11th power = 2048. Subtract those two naughty addresses and you have 2046 valid addresses per subnet.

199.17.30.0 255.255.255.248

That mask is /29 in prefix notation. 32 – 29 = 3 host bits. 2 to the 3rd power = 8; subtract the 2 and you have six valid addresses per subnet.

47.0.0.0 /255.255.255.128

That mask is /25 in prefix notation. 32 – 25 = 7 host bits. (2 to the 7th power – 2) = 126 valid addresses per subnet.

Calculate the broadcast address and range of valid addresses for each of these subnets.
- 18.0.0.0 /17
- 130.214.64.0 /21
- 216.189.37.128 /26
- 214.37.19.192 /27
- 99.0.0.0 255.252.0.0
- 120.47.32.0 255.255.248.0

18.0.0.0 /17:

	Octet 1	Octet 2	Octet 3	Octet 4
Subnet Address, All host bits set to zero.	00010010	00000000	0**0000000**	**00000000**
B'Cast Address, all host bits set to one.	00010010	00000000	0**1111111**	**1111111**

Subnet address: 18.0.0.0 /17

Range of valid addresses: 18.0.0.1 – 18.0.127.254 /17

Broadcast address: 18.0.127.255 /17

130.214.64.0 /21:

	Octet 1	Octet 2	Octet 3	Octet 4
Subnet Address, All host bits set to zero.	10000010	11010110	01000**000**	**00000000**
B'Cast Address, all host bits set to one.	10000010	11010110	01000**111**	**11111111**

Subnet address: 130.214.64.0 /21

Range of valid addresses: 130.214.64.1 – 130.214.71.254 /21

Broadcast address: 130.214.71.255 /21

216.189.37.128 /26

	Octet 1	Octet 2	Octet 3	Octet 4
Subnet Address, All host bits set to zero.	11011000	10111101	00100101	10**000000**
B'Cast Address, all host bits set to one.	11011000	10111101	00100101	10**111111**

Subnet address: 216.189.37.128 /26

Range of valid addresses: 216.189.37.129 – 216.189.37.190 / 26

Broadcast address: 216.189.37.191 /26

214.37.19.192 /27:

	Octet 1	Octet 2	Octet 3	Octet 4
Subnet Address, All host bits set to zero.	11010110	00100101	00010011	110**00000**
B'Cast Address, all host bits set to one.	11010110	00100101	00010011	110**11111**

Subnet address: 214.37.19.192 /27

Range of valid addresses: 214.37.19.193 – 214.37.19.222 /27

Broadcast address: 214.37.19.223 /27

99.0.0.0 255.252.0.0:

	Octet 1	Octet 2	Octet 3	Octet 4
Subnet Address, All host bits set to zero.	01100011	000000**00**	**00000000**	**00000000**
B'Cast Address, all host bits set to one.	01100011	000000**11**	**11111111**	**11111111**

Subnet address: 99.0.0.0 255.252.0.0 (/14)

Range of valid addresses: 99.0.0.1 – 99.3.255.254 255.252.0.0

Broadcast address: 99.3.255.255 255.252.0.0

120.47.32.0 255.255.248.0:

	Octet 1	Octet 2	Octet 3	Octet 4
Subnet Address, All host bits set to zero.	01111000	00101111	00100**000**	**00000000**
B'Cast Address, all host bits set to one.	01111000	00101111	00100**111**	**11111111**

Subnet address: 120.47.32.0 255.255.248.0 (/21)

Range of valid addresses: 120.47.32.1 – 120.47.39.254 255.255.248.0

Broadcast address: 120.47.39.255 255.255.248.0

We'll wrap things up with a little more subnetting!

You're subnetting the 200.14.39.0 network, and you need at least 32 host addresses per subnet. You also want to maximize the number of available subnets. What's the best mask for the job?

With this Class C network, we begin with eight host bits.

	1st Octet	2nd Octet	3rd Octet	4th Octet
Network Bits	11111111	11111111	11111111	
Subnet Bits				
Host Bits				00000000

We'll need at least six host bits to have 32 valid addresses (2 to the 6th power – 2 = 62). That means we can borrow only two host bits for subnetting, leaving us with the mask 255.255.255.192 (/26) and a total of four subnets and 62 valid addresses per subnet.

	1st Octet	2nd Octet	3rd Octet	4th Octet
Network Bits	11111111	11111111	11111111	
Subnet Bits				11
Host Bits				000000

You're subnetting the 150.17.0.0 network, and you have two requirements for the subnet mask. First, it must result in at least 100 valid subnets being available. Second, there must be between 50 and 150 valid hosts on every resulting subnet. What mask or masks, if any, will accomplish this?

With this Class B network, we begin with sixteen network bits and sixteen host bits.

	1st Octet	2nd Octet	3rd Octet	4th Octet
Network Bits	11111111	11111111		
Subnet Bits				
Host Bits			00000000	00000000

To meet the subnet requirement, we'd have to borrow at least seven host bits for subnetting. That would result in 128 valid subnets (2 to the 7th power).

	1st Octet	2nd Octet	3rd Octet	4th Octet
Network Bits	11111111	11111111		
Subnet Bits			1111111	
Host Bits			0	00000000

This 255.255.254.0 mask meets the first requirement, but not the second. Those nine remaining host bits result in 510 addresses per subnet (2 to the 9th power – 2), so we can't use this mask.

Borrowing one more host bit gives us well over 100 subnets. Does it meet the second requirement?

	1st Octet	2nd Octet	3rd Octet	4th Octet
Network Bits	11111111	11111111		
Subnet Bits			11111111	
Host Bits				00000000

Nope! While we do meet the first requirement, we still have too many hosts per subnet (2 to the 8th power – 2 = 254). Let's borrow one more bit and see what happens.

	1st Octet	2nd Octet	3rd Octet	4th Octet
Network Bits	11111111	11111111		
Subnet Bits			11111111	1
Host Bits				0000000

The 255.255.255.128 mask results in 512 valid subnets (2 to the 9th power) and 126 valid addresses per subnet (2 to the 7th power – 2). The /25 mask is a winner. What about the /26 mask?

	1st Octet	2nd Octet	3rd Octet	4th Octet
Network Bits	11111111	11111111		
Subnet Bits			11111111	11
Host Bits				000000

The 255.255.255.192 mask results in *way* over 100 subnets (1024, to be exact) and 62 valid addresses per subnet (2 to the 6th power – 2). That meets both requirements.

Let's go one step further and see what happens with the /27 mask.

	1st Octet	2nd Octet	3rd Octet	4th Octet
Network Bits	11111111	11111111		
Subnet Bits			11111111	111
Host Bits				00000

With this mask, we end up with 2048 valid subnets (2 to the 11th power, natch) and 30 valid addresses per subnet (2 to the 5th power – 2). We only meet one requirement, so we can't use this mask. The winning masks are /25 and /26.

Given the 161.64.0.0 network, what subnet mask or masks (if any) will result in having at least 500 subnets and at least 100 users per subnet?

With any and all Class B networks, we begin with 16 host bits ripe for borrowing for subnetting.

	1st Octet	2nd Octet	3rd Octet	4th Octet
Network Bits	11111111	11111111		
Subnet Bits				
Host Bits			00000000	00000000

The lowest number of subnet bits that results in at least 500 subnets is nine (2 to the 9th power = 512). That would leave seven host bits, which gives us 126 valid addresses on each of those subnets. The mask 255.255.255.128 (/25) meets both requirements.

	1st Octet	2nd Octet	3rd Octet	4th Octet
Network Bits	11111111	11111111		
Subnet Bits			11111111	1
Host Bits				0000000

That's the only mask that meets both requirements. If we borrow one more bit for subnetting, we end up with 1024 valid subnets (2 to the 10th power) but only 62 valid addresses on each subnet (2 to the 6th power – 2). The one and only winning mask is 255.255.255.128 (/25).

You're subnetting the 33.0.0.0 network and you've got some big numbers to work with in your requirements. You need at least 1138 subnets and at least 2023 valid IP addresses on each subnet. What mask or masks (if any) will accomplish this?

With our Class A network, we begin with a whopping 24 host bits.

	1st Octet	2nd Octet	3rd Octet	4th Octet
Network Bits	11111111			
Subnet Bits				
Host Bits		00000000	00000000	00000000

For at least 1138 subnets, we need to borrow at least 11 host bits for subnetting. That gives us 2048 subnets and leaves 13 host bits, which results in 8190 addresses per subnet (2 to the 13th power – 2). The 255.255.224.0 (/19) mask meets both requirements.

	1st Octet	2nd Octet	3rd Octet	4th Octet
Network Bits	11111111			
Subnet Bits		11111111	111	
Host Bits			00000	00000000

If we borrow one more host bit, the resulting 255.255.240.0 (/20) mask gives us 4096 subnets and 4094 valid addresses per subnet (2 to the 12th power and 2 to the 12th power – 2, respectively). This mask also works.

	1st Octet	2nd Octet	3rd Octet	4th Octet
Network Bits	11111111			
Subnet Bits		11111111	1111	
Host Bits			0000	00000000

Borrowing yet another host bit gives us 8192 subnets (2 to the 13th power), but the number of valid addresses per subnet declines to 2046 (2 to the 11th power – 2). The mask 255.255.248.0 (/21) also works, but it's likely the last one that does.

	1st Octet	2nd Octet	3rd Octet	4th Octet
Network Bits	11111111			
Subnet Bits		11111111	11111	
Host Bits			000	00000000

Borrowing one *more* host bit gives us over 16,000 valid subnets (2 to the 14th power = 16,384), but as you'd suspect, the resulting number of hosts per subnet isn't coming close to the requirement. The remaining ten host bits give us 1022 IP addresses per subnet (2 to the 10th power – 2), which fails to meet the second requirement, so the 255.255.255.252 (/22) mask doesn't work.

	1st Octet	2nd Octet	3rd Octet	4th Octet
Network Bits	11111111			
Subnet Bits		11111111	111111	
Host Bits			00	00000000

The winning masks are /19, /20, and /21.

Thanks again for purchasing this book – I appreciate it! -- Chris B.

Made in the USA
Monee, IL
14 August 2020